ROOKIE SEASON

A Year with the West Michigan Whitecaps

BRANSON WRIGHT

WILLIAM B. EERDMANS PUBLISHING COMPANY
GRAND RAPIDS, MICHIGAN

PUBLISHER'S NOTE

In 1994 the *Grand Rapids Press* assigned sports reporter Branson Wright to cover the inaugural season of the West Michigan Whitecaps. The *Press* was the only newspaper in the country to provide daily coverage of a Class A minor league team both at home and away. Much of the material in this book is excerpted from articles first published in the *Press* as part of Wright's Whitecaps coverage. The publisher gratefully acknowledges the permission of the *Grand Rapids Press* to reprint this material.

A portion of the proceeds from the sale of this book will go toward the Santa Claus Girls, a Grand Rapids community charity that the *Press* has long supported.

© 1995 Wm. B. Eerdmans Publishing Co.
255 Jefferson Ave. S.E., Grand Rapids, Michigan 49503
All rights reserved

Printed in the United States of America

00 99 98 97 96 95   7 6 5 4 3 2 1

Library of Congress Cataloging-in-Publication Data

Wright, Branson, 1963-
   Rookie season: a year with the West Michigan Whitecaps / Branson Wright.
      p.   cm.
   ISBN 0-8028-7057-0 (pbk.: alk. paper)
   1. West Michigan Whitecaps (Baseball team) I. Title.
GV875.W47W75   1995
796.357'09774 — dc20   95-11868
                                          CIP

Contents

Acknowledgments	vii
Introduction	viii
ROOKIE SEASON	1
Player Profiles	173
Team Statistics	193

This book is dedicated to author Alex Haley and actor Ron Taylor

Acknowledgments

The completion of this book would not have been possible without God, the support of my wife Kendra, the spirit of my mother Alice Davis, and the mentoring of Charles Storey and Ken Simonson. Special thanks to Bob Becker and the *Grand Rapids Press* and to everyone at Wm. B. Eerdmans Publishing Co.

I also thank Lori Clark of the Whitecaps for providing the statistics included in this work.

This book is in honor of the houseful of friends who never doubted me during the rough times: Bryan Allen, Charles Fowler, Raymond Hambrick, John Holifield, Montoya Holston, Boyzell Hosey, Kevin Huhn, Kenny McKinnie, Rodney McKissic, Davis Miller, Geoff Neville, Tyrone Powers, Scott Sims, Tim Smith, Ron Thomas, Larry Whiteside, Ron Wright, and Haki Zuberi.

Introduction

West Michigan Whitecaps general partner Lew Chamberlin couldn't quite believe what he saw through his wire-framed glasses that frigid winter morning on March 5, 1994. More than one thousand baseball-starved fans lined up around an entire block leading to the front door of his office. It was only 8 A.M., and the doors weren't scheduled to open to sell opening day tickets for another two hours. To get a jump on the competition, more than twenty-five crazed fans had camped out in the blistering cold the night before.

"When I drove up that morning all I could see was a stretch of people doing the wave and having a good time," Chamberlin said. "I have to admit, my eyes misted over a little bit."

Chamberlin's eyes continued to mist over throughout the entire baseball season as the fans continued to flock to Old Kent Park. The Whitecaps (affiliated with the Oakland Athletics) shattered the Midwest League attendance record on August 9, when more than 8,000 fans brought the season total to 361,722 at that point. The league mark stood at 354,327, set in 1993 by the Kane County club. The following week on August 16, the Whitecaps reached 400,000 to become only the second Class A franchise in the history of professional baseball to achieve that mark. Finally on September 1, the Whitecaps smashed the all-time Class A season attendance record set by Denver (463,039) in 1949.

General partner Lew Chamberlin fulfilled his dream of bringing professional baseball to West Michigan.
Courtesy the *Grand Rapids Press*.

"This was a fairy tale year," said West Michigan general manager Scott Lane. "When we got started, we projected 300,000 to 350,000 fans for the entire year. What we did this year really says something about the community."

The community and the West Michigan franchise were rewarded with the 1995 Midwest League All-Star game because of their effort. "That was easy," said league president George Spelius. "Lew Chamberlin and Scott Lane did a fantastic job this year. The response they received from the fans in West Michigan was beyond my expectations. They had a superb year."

◆ ◆ ◆

It took ten years of preparation to get ready for the kind of year West Michigan had in 1994. Chamberlin's family had sold their steel supply company in 1985, and he began looking at other business opportunities.

Chamberlin was interested in bringing minor league baseball to Grand Rapids. So was Dennis Baxter, an accountant based in Muskegon. Baseball executives recommended that Chamberlin and Baxter get together. With some partners, the two bought the Wausau (Wisconsin) Timbers of the Midwest League, eventually moving the team to suburban Chicago. That team, the Kane County Cougars, became successful with the help of a new stadium and aggressive marketing. But despite their success there, Chamberlin and Baxter still wanted to bring a team home to Grand Rapids.

With a group of prominent business leaders, Baxter and Chamberlin then bought the Madison (Wisconsin) Muskies, also of the Midwest League. In 1993 they received approval to move the franchise to Grand Rapids and sold their interest in Kane County. About this same time, West Michigan Baseball Inc. announced a blockbuster. It was building a privately financed, $6 million, 5,700 seat stadium. The majority of the funding would come from a local bank, Old Kent Bank, for which the ball park would later be named. A regional contest provided the team's nickname — Whitecaps, from the crests of waves on Lake Michigan, forty miles from Grand Rapids.

◆ ◆ ◆

Snow covered the ground in January, and the stadium was far from completion, but West Michigan sold two thousand season tickets. Sixteen of twenty luxury boxes at fifteen thousand dollars each were sold, and billboard space under the scoreboard and along the outfield fence went for an average of five thousand dollars per sign.

Nearly a thousand Whitecaps fans brave the elements to purchase opening day tickets. Courtesy the *Grand Rapids Press*.

And just when Baxter and Chamberlin thought nothing could top already brisk sales, they witnessed a host of area residents braving the West Michigan winter to stand in line for opening day tickets. The response was so great that the game was quickly sold out, and several hundred fans had to be turned away.

During spring training, the future Whitecaps caught a glimpse of the front page photo in the *Grand Rapids Press* showing the throng of fans lined up for tickets. This was just a hint of what the season would bring. "We were told how excited the fans were going to be this year, but no one expected crowds of eight thousand," said Whitecaps pitcher Matt Walsh. "It's been a real pleasure to play at Old Kent Park."

Whitecaps manager Jim Colborn, who pitched for ten years in the major leagues, hated for the season to end because of the warmth he received from the park. "Little by little, as the season went on at Old Kent Park, it felt more like home," Colborn said. "It felt more like home than my apartment, the team bus, or any hotel. The fans were like my family. It was so much fun hearing the people. I really enjoyed it."

Catcher Willie Morales said the fan support was key to the final surge at the end of the season. "We're entertainers, and we're performing for the people as well as for ourselves," Morales said. "Anytime there are people out in the crowd it makes it a lot better for the players. When you do good things and people see it, they remember you for a long time."

Added outfielder Mat Reese, "Playing at Old Kent Park gave you an idea of what it's like to play at higher levels. The fans were great all year in supporting us."

Outfielder D. T. Cromer, who as a Madison Muskie in 1993 played at often empty Warner Park, got an extra jolt at Old Kent Park. "Large crowds make it more exciting," Cromer said. "In Madison you had to go out and play for yourself and have the desire to play the game. If you were down (emotionally) at Old Kent Park, you had the fans to bring you up."

◆ ◆ ◆

Before the home fans could get the players excited, the Whitecaps had to open the season on the road at South Bend. The game was one of ten shown live on television back in Grand Rapids, but many fans couldn't wait to see their new team in person.

A week after tickets for the home opener sold out, two local radio stations organized a bus trip to South Bend. For forty dollars, fans received transportation to and from South Bend, a game ticket, and an inaugural season baseball cap. The promotion was so popular that the stations had to schedule three buses, each carrying forty-seven passengers, and had to cut off reservations earlier than anticipated.

When the team returned to West Michigan for opening day, Lori Clark, who handles public relations for the Whitecaps, had to limit media requests to cover the game. "This year was beyond my wildest dreams," said Clark, who worked for the Chattanooga Lookouts and the Madison Muskies prior to coming to the Whitecaps. "I had 150 media requests for opening day from all over the state. The media coverage has been good all year. The team was covered by a local newspaper home and away, along with home and road radio coverage. Two local television stations gave us coverage throughout the season."

Opening day was sold out, but the beat didn't stop there. Attendance at Old Kent Park topped 8,000 fans eighteen times during the season, and averaged 6,988 fans per game. The response made a ticket to Old Kent Park a hot item.

"It was an unbelievable response in terms of ticket sales," said ticket manager Bruce Radley. "It was very difficult to turn people away when there weren't any more tickets. There were

West Michigan fans get their first look at the team in the road opener at South Bend. Courtesy the *Grand Rapids Press*.

times on the weekends that we had to turn hundreds of people away. This was a ticket manager's dream, because we didn't have to sit around idle just hoping someone would buy tickets."

The West Michigan organization planned to do everything it could to satisfy its fans. Plans were made to add more seats for the following season. One popular attraction already was the availablity of lawn seats. For three dollars a fan could bring a blanket or a lawn chair and have a picnic on the grass and watch a baseball game during the warmth of the summer.

"Obviously people wanted baseball, but I believe the facility had something to do with the enthusiasm," said Jim Jarecki, director of baseball operations. "When the fans came here, they got good baseball and family entertainment. They kept coming back because they were having a good time."

ROOKIE SEASON

Spring Training

You can't avoid the simmering rays from the sun. The glare and the heat have a way of getting your attention, especially when the temperature in Arizona reaches 90 degrees in late March. Several hundred green and gold uniformed figures in the distance appear to ignore the pressure cooker–like heat while tooling in the field. The small patches of sweat on their jersey tops are the only indication of reaction to the steamy temperature.

Scottsdale Community College sits neatly on 160 acres of land. The college is surrounded by the McDowell Mountains, which provide shade from the sun in the evenings. The twenty-five-year-old community college in Scottsdale is leasing the land from the Salt River-Pima Maricopa Native American community. The school has a student enrollment of ten thousand, and since 1983 the Oakland Athletics major league baseball team has increased the population on campus with the spring training of their minor league clubs. One of those clubs is their Class A team. After being known for years as the Madison Muskies, the team would now be called the West Michigan Whitecaps, because the franchise had been relocated.

This is where it all began. Twenty-five players, one manager, a pitching coach, and a trainer would all leave Arizona and begin a quest to be a part of Class A minor league history in their very first season.

Manager Jim Colborn successfully piloted the Whitecaps through their first season. Courtesy the *Grand Rapids Press*.

The Skipper

Weeks before Jim Colborn went to his first spring training as manager of the West Michigan Whitecaps, he already knew how he wanted to run his ship.

"My philosophy is for players to play their best and become better in an environment where they're not afraid to make mistakes," Colborn said. "My first goal this spring is for them to play aggressively, have fun, and play without the fear of making mistakes. Under those circumstances, people perform their best."

Colborn himself performed his best during a ten-year major league pitching career, but not without a mix of hijinks and shenanigans. In fact, Colborn was considered a flake during his four-year stint (1972-76) with the Milwaukee Brewers. Back then, Colborn liked to impersonate ball boys, umpires, and members of the grounds crew. Once he dressed up as the Milwaukee team mascot, Bernie Brewer, and slid down the chute into a giant mug of balloons. Rumor has it that he also streaked on the team bus.

Mike Hegan, a former Brewer infielder, reflected on one of Colborn's antics. "I'm standing out in left field, and the ground crew comes out to do the field," Hegan told the *Milwaukee Sentinel* in June 1994. "And here's this guy in lederhosen (a short German-style outfit with suspenders).

"As he gets closer, I see the zipper scar across his knees from operations, and I know it's Colborn. I'd like to see a player pull something like that today. They'd call security. They'd set up an appointment with a shrink."

Colborn pitched some of his best years in Milwaukee. In 1973, he became the Brewers' first twenty-game winner and was named to the American League All-Star team. That was the same year he pitched in 314 innings, a record that still stands.

Colborn hopes the record will overshadow the shenanigans in his past. "I'm a little embarrassed for my players to read about what I did, because it has been taken out of context a little," Colborn said with the half smile that would become familiar to players, fans, and media during the season ahead. "I was doing light-hearted humor to help everyone enjoy life."

Colborn has enjoyed life, winning eighty-three games pitching for the Chicago Cubs, Brewers, Kansas City Royals, and Seattle Mariners. He won eighteen games with the Royals in 1977, including the no-hitter he tossed against the Texas Rangers on May 14. Colborn earned a bachelor of arts degree in sociology from Whittier (California) College. He also did graduate work at the University of Washington and one year of graduate studies at the University of Edinburgh in Scotland. In 1969, Colborn married Jennifer Sands, and four children followed — Daisy, Rose, Holly, and Jimmy, Jr.

But Colborn's life didn't seem so enjoyable when he wasn't drafted to play pro ball after college graduation. "I looked in the *L.A. Times* and didn't see my name in the draft," Colborn remembered. "I thought, 'Oh well, I guess I'm not good enough,' so I decided to get a job or go to graduate school."

While contemplating which direction he'd take his life, a pro tryout was arranged. A scout came out and watched the right-hander pitch to one of his teammates. That close look was followed by a closer look. Colborn was invited to pitch for the Cubs minor league team in the California League.

"I did well," Colborn recalled. "I pitched five innings and struck out ten of fifteen batters. The only hit was a fly ball in the sun. The scouts were impressed and signed me for a four-hundred-dollar bonus."

Gordon Goldsberry, now a special assistant to the general

manager of the Baltimore Orioles, was the scout who signed Colborn. He glows with delight when the subject of Colborn is brought up. "I first saw him in college," Goldsberry said. "He probably didn't get drafted because he didn't throw very hard. As a scout, you wanted to see a guy that could throw in the high 80s. Colborn couldn't, but he had great command.

"I was impressed with his intelligence and competitive nature and his willingness to listen to ideas. I'm very proud of his success. He made his career on his own. He performed and did an outstanding job."

Two years after Colborn signed, he found himself with the big league club. He felt like a child in wonderland. "I'd never been in a major league camp," Colborn reflected. "I didn't know the players on the Cubs. I'd heard of them, but I'd never met them."

Colborn joined a team with legendary manager Leo Durocher and Hall of Famers Ernie Banks, Ron Santo, and Billy Williams. "I only knew them from listening to Dodger broadcasts when Vin Scully would say something about the Cubs. I hadn't the slightest idea of what to expect. All I could do was throw a baseball where it was supposed to be thrown."

Colborn spent three years with the Cubs, followed by four years with the Brewers. In 1977 with the Royals, he had the biggest day in his baseball life. "I hadn't been pitching well prior to that day," Colborn said. "I remember having trouble in the third inning. I remember saying to myself sarcastically, 'You went through three innings without giving up a hit for a change.'

"George Brett asked how I felt. He'd usually say, 'You look good. Keep it up.' But this day he was saying I was throwing terrible and to keep it up! Brett said it again in the ninth inning when no one else would talk to me or even look at me. He had the courage to tell that same joke. It made me relax." Colborn went on to record his first no-hitter.

Colborn's playing days ended with the Seattle Mariners after the 1979 season. For five years, his life took on a new look. He returned home to Ventura, California, where he became a real estate salesman.

The itch to return to the game, however, overcame him. From 1984-89, Colborn rejoined the Cubs minor league system as a pitching instructor and coordinator. Once his thirst was quenched, he was ready to run some more.

Colborn was interested in travelling to a foreign country to experience some more international baseball. In college, Colborn was part of a contingency of players that competed in Europe. He learned that a team in Japan was looking for a pitching coach, and what initially was planned as a tour became a four-year stint with the Orix Blue Wave of the Pacific League.

The pay for a pitching coach in Japan is double the salary of a major league manager in the States. That was the easy thing to get used to. Adjusting to the culture was another matter. "The language was a barrier, and I sprinted to learn Japanese as quickly as I could," Colborn said. "I carried a book with me at all times, and I had an interpreter. But one fall camp, I didn't have an interpreter, and not one person there spoke English.

"The Japanese don't understand self-deprecating humor. When you make fun of yourself, they don't understand — and I do that a lot. They don't understand sarcasm like we do over here."

The Japanese culture is also woven into baseball alongside the stitches. The rule are basically the same, but Colborn said the important thing to the Japanese is not who wins, but how you play the game. "They have games that end in ties after twelve innings. In another league it's fifteen innings," Colborn said. "Over there you had to practice very hard with all of your heart and soul, like a true Samurai. If your practice gets rained out, you can't have the (scheduled) game because the preparation is all part of the contest.

"When that happened to me the first time, it took a while to realize what was happening, because competition and whether you win or lose is everything in America. That was the core of a lot of misunderstanding."

When Colborn's contract with the Blue Wave ran out, he was eager to remain in the game after returning to the States. His name was mentioned to the Oakland Athletics, and it was then that he was offered the job to manage West Michigan.

Gil Patterson

The snickers and grins were hard to miss throughout the Scottsdale Community College complex. Here was Whitecaps pitching instructor Gil Patterson trying to demonstrate pitching techniques to his players, but they were obviously distracted.

"Everyone's laughing at me," said Patterson, who was reduced to crutches and an ankle brace after breaking his ankle during a roller-skating spill in February. "When I'm demonstrating drills, everyone's teasing me because I look like Tim Conway doing miniature golf. I'm on my knees doing my exercises, trying to demonstrate, and the players are laughing because I look like I'm losing my balance."

But Patterson never lost his enthusiasm. "That's what's so funny about it," said Whitecaps pitcher Steve Lemke.

"We're so used to seeing him really involved while teaching. He has so much energy, and I know the crutches and the brace are driving him nuts."

Ironically, injuries are what got Patterson involved in coaching. He was drafted four times from high school through junior college, and he finally signed a contract with the New York Yankees in 1975. Patterson was 24-6 on the minor league level. However, he injured his shoulder after pitching more than three hundred innings for two consecutive years.

In the spring of 1977, Patterson made it to the majors with the Yankees, but he left his arm in the minors. "My usual fastball of 90 to 95 mph and my control were gone," he reflected. "It was like a knife was in my shoulder. It was the beginning of the end."

Patterson remained with the parent club, but he was put on the disabled list twice during that year. His troubles were compounded because he thought that if he was going to stay in the majors he would have to keep pitching. "I tore my rotator cuff," said Patterson, pointing to his right shoulder. "I had eight operations over the next eight years."

Atlanta Braves manager Bobby Cox was in the New York Yankees organization during the mid 1970s. In 1976, Cox managed Class AAA Syracuse. In 1977, he was the first base coach for the parent club. "Gil (Patterson) was a super prospect," said Cox about the Whitecaps pitching coach. "He had great stuff. I saw him as a big league pitcher with some great years, but he hurt his arm. He was one of those few guys that came along who was going to be really good. He had a real good fastball and an outstanding breaking ball. He had it all."

Patterson gave it all up for a new choice — exit playing days, enter teaching days. Patterson teamed up and worked with former Yankee star Bucky Dent at a baseball school in Florida. After a brief stint there, he was hired by the Oakland A's and was sent to Scottsdale to work with players on the

Rookie level. He worked on that level for two years before moving on to Madison in 1993. The following season he joined Jim Colborn.

"You get so much satisfaction out of playing, but you can get almost as much by helping players develop," Patterson said. Patterson hoped his approach would satisfy his pitchers. He wanted to mesh the physical and mental aspects of pitching.

"The physical approach, of course, is the mechanics," Patterson said. "If people can stay healthy, they'll have a chance at pitching in the big leagues. I try to do everything I can to water that seed." Patterson said the mental approach is based on confidence — "having players believe in themselves and get them thinking that they can get it done, no matter what happens."

The Class A-level teams in the Oakland A's minor league system have been experimenting with four sets of two pitchers, who pair off as part of the rotation. For example, the Whitecaps carried twelve pitchers to Grand Rapids, eight starting pitchers and four in relief. The eight starting pitchers were paired off, one lefty and one righty. Each tandem flip-flopped between starts, with the pair alternating between opening the game and following in relief.

"We have lots of good quality arms," Patterson explained. "With a normal staff you have five starters and seven in the bullpen. Those five starters are happy because they'll get 130 to 140 innings in, pitching every five days.

"The eight-man staff allows pitchers on both levels (of Class A) to throw 120, 130, or 150 innings during the season," Patterson said. "There's no concern of overwork because they'll throw every four days, and they'll pitch a limit of seventy pitches (each game), no matter how many innings it takes. Then the other pitcher will come in. They'll also flip-flop starts."

"Doc"

The Whitecaps' field staff also included Brian "Doc" Thorson. Thorson, like Patterson, came over from the Madison franchise. Although Thorson's title with the Whitecaps was trainer, his duties went far beyond wraps and rubbing alcohol.

First there was Thorson the hotel coordinator. Thorson was responsible for making sure the rooms were set up before the team arrived at specific destinations on the road. Then there was Thorson the restaurant manager. On the road, Thorson made sure the players had pregame meals in the clubhouse. There was also Thorson the laundry man and Thorson the movie man. Thorson provided video rentals for the players on the team bus, which was equipped with a VCR. But no matter which title Thorson held, to the Whitecaps he remained the "Doc."

"I just have so much respect for that guy," said Whitecaps pitcher Zack Sawyer, who was with Thorson on the Madison team in the 1993 season. "He goes through what we go through. He rides the bus and gets up even earlier than we do. He has a lot of respect for his job. Day in and day out, he's there for us. I can always count on 'Doc.' But we always rag on him every now and then, because he's one of us."

Thorson has been a part of the Oakland Athletics organization for eleven of his sixteen years as a trainer. He's had stints in Madison and Class AA Huntsville.

No matter where he's worked, Doc's main responsibility is the same — the care and prevention of athletic injuries. "A trainer is just the first step for a player," Thorson said. "I may take an injured player to the doctor, where he'll have his basic tests. Then that information is relayed to Oakland, where they'll decide what's best for the player." That could include rehab at the spring training complex in Arizona, where a

David Keel, Doc Thorson, and Steve Cox congratulate Randy Ortega. Courtesy the *Grand Rapids Press*.

physical therapist is on staff, or the player could visit one of the doctors who work regularly within the organization. The player could also be sent back home, where he may feel more comfortable during his rehabilitation process. Thorson is also responsible for keeping the A's organization updated daily on player injuries.

Thorson spent his first five years in baseball with the Milwaukee Brewers, where he had the opportunity to work as an assistant trainer during the 1992 World Series. He has also spent eight winter seasons as head trainer for the Puerto Rican League team in Mayaguez, where he leaves some fond memories.

During one particular winter, Thorson's team had a one

and one-half game lead on the second place team for the final playoff spot. Even though Thorson's club lost the first of their remaining games, they thought they were still assured a division title because of a heavy rain that would prevent making up a previously suspended game.

How wrong they were. "The rain stopped, but the field was too wet to play," Thorson remembered. "Then all of a sudden, I looked out in center field and here came trucks with gasoline barrels. They poured gas on the field and set it on fire. It was like a big bonfire."

Thorson, who earned his health education degree from the University of Wisconsin-LaCrosse, would also like to forget the transportation in those days. "One time the bus driver ran fifty-two red lights after a game," said Thorson, who resides in Madison, Wisconsin. "I take off my glasses as we're climbing this huge hill. I put them back on and notice we're going down this hill on the wrong side of the road. We get down to the end, and the driver changes lanes at the intersection like nothing's going on. Winter ball is one heck of a ride."

Latin Ball Players

Before and after spring training exhibition games, ball players from the same hometowns will get together and talk about old times. Often these are players from the same state or the same region. To meet someone with a similar background is always refreshing when you're many hours from home, especially when you're adjusting to a new climate or language.

Since the 1960s the Oakland organization has been aggressive in signing and developing players from Latin American countries. In the Dominican Republic, the A's have established a firm grip on scouting and developing talent with the addition of a training facility there and with the help of Hall of Famer Juan Marichal as director of Latin American scouting.

In the past, the A's would bring the Latin American players to developmental ball in Scottsdale after one or two years in the Dominican. With the new training complex, the organization can now keep them in the Dominican a little longer, and then players could move directly from there to Grand Rapids. Previously, they would spend another couple of years in Scottsdale getting acclimated to this region.

"The biggest adjustment they make is leaving a warm

Jose Guillen and Juan Dilone warm up.   Courtesy the *Grand Rapids Press.*

climate in their country to a similar climate in Arizona, and then they are shocked if they're sent to a Grand Rapids," said Keith Lieppman, director of player development for the A's. "They have a long time getting adjusted to that."

Along with helping the Latin American players refine their baseball skills, the Dominican complex is also used to help the players in other ways. "We have English classes that we start down there," Lieppman said. "We also teach them about proper diet, writing checks, and how to rent furniture."

◆ ◆ ◆

One of the by-products of the Dominican complex is Juan Dilone. "He's one of the few that came over here that learned quickly," Lieppman said. "He's a very intelligent kid."

Dilone (pronounced Dee-low-NAY) is one of three Dominicans who left spring training with the Whitecaps. The others are infielders Vicente (also known as Vinny) Francisco and Jose Guillen.

Unlike many Latin players, Dilone was fortunate to attend college in the Dominican Republic. This is where he studied English. The younger Dominican players in the A's minor league system look to Dilone for guidance. "They look up to me like a big brother," Dilone said. "They can't speak English as well as I can, so they'll ask me many questions. Sometimes they'll need help with the menu in restaurants, or they'll ask how they'll be treated by people in the street."

He remembers his own fears when he first arrived in the States three years ago. "The language was the biggest problem," said Dilone, who's from Santo Domingo. "I had to remember to speak English slowly, because maybe someone wouldn't understand me. It can be scary adjusting to a different place."

Dilone, a switch hitter, spent a season at the complex in the Dominican. In 1991 and 1992 he played Rookie ball in

Scottsdale. Last year he played with Southern Oregon in the Northwest League.

Manager Jim Colborn said Dilone's English is a plus, but he's not playing with the Whitecaps because of his bilingual abilities. "He has some nice skills," Colborn said. "He has a good bat and he can play several (infield) positions. He's a switch hitter with a little power. He'll probably hit a lot of extra base hits, not necessarily for home run power, but he's the kind of guy who hits everything from homers and doubles to triples."

There isn't much of a barrier for the Latin players when it comes to understanding the language of baseball. Dilone said the baseball lingo is basically the same in Spanish and English except for the pronunciation. One baseball term that is different from Spanish to English is "strikeout." In Spanish a strikeout is called *bonche* (pronounced bone-CHEY).

"You begin to understand your orders in the field once you're told the same thing over and over again during spring training," Dilone said. "You'll catch on easily."

When Dilone returns home in the off season, he's often asked the same list of questions. "How is the States, do you play in a big ball park, how are the people, do the women look like the ones on Soul Train?" Dilone said. "Everyone in the Dominican thinks the United States is a great place."

Other than the weather change, Dilone enjoys his stay in the States. "The weather in the Dominican and Arizona is the same. But when you go to other places like Michigan, it's colder. The other (Dominican) players always ask me about the weather."

Usually Dilone will share with them his first experience with snow. "The first time I saw snow, I was visiting some relatives in New York," Dilone said. "I thought it was great. I ran outside looking up in the sky wondering what in the heck was going on."

Jeff D'Amico, Whitecaps' Top Choice

When Michael Jordan made his leap into minor league baseball after a stellar basketball career, his critics came at him from all angles. But tuning out the criticism was a gifted shortstop who shared the same dreams as Jordan.

"I think it's pretty cool," said Jeff D'Amico, Oakland's second-round pick in the 1993 draft. "I'm sure there are probably some outfielders mad about it because they feel he's taken their job. But if you look at him as a scout would, you'd see that he has a chance because he's a good athlete. Give him a year, and I'll bet he does alright."

D'Amico denies it, but because of his own background, it was understandable why his heart went out to the former NBA superstar. Last year, D'Amico was a two-sport high school star for Redmond High School in Redmond, Washington. He led his team to the Class AAA basketball final four, where they lost in the semifinals. The six-foot-three D'Amico averaged sixteen points per game and was named second-team all-state.

In baseball, D'Amico led Redmond to a state championship victory. At the plate he batted over .450, and he was 10-0 as a pitcher in the last half of the season. He also pitched a thrilling 2-1, nine-inning victory in the state championship final. D'Amico was named first-team all-state in baseball.

After enjoying success in dual sports, D'Amico accepted a baseball and basketball scholarship to UCLA during the early signing period in November 1992. He was drafted by the Oakland A's in the second round of the 1993 June free agent draft. D'Amico had a decision to make. His girlfriend accepted a softball scholarship to UCLA, and here was his chance to play two sports at the same school. But as always, including this case, money talked, and you know what walked.

"It was still a tough decision," said D'Amico, who signed a $190,000 bonus in August of that year. "My parents are college oriented. Getting an education was important to them." Oakland accommodated D'Amico by including money for his education in his contract. In the offseason he planned to attend UCLA.

After signing the contract, D'Amico headed for Rookie ball for the Southern Oregon club. In thirty-three games last season, he batted .263, cracked three homers, and drove in fifteen runs. Once that season ended in September, D'Amico spent two weeks in instructional ball.

The rigors of minor league baseball for D'Amico were a far cry from the high energy level of basketball. "I'll miss it (basketball)," said D'Amico, whose father, Tom, played in the Los Angeles Dodgers minor league organization during the late 1960s and early 1970s. "There's nothing like the competitiveness of basketball. Baseball is a lot more time consuming."

D'Amico also pointed out that baseball forces one to develop a different type of discipline. "No matter how you feel or what the weather is like," D'Amico said, "you have to be ready to play in 140 games. The longevity is what I've had to prepare for."

Keith Lieppman, director of player development, liked what he'd seen of D'Amico this spring. "For us to send a high school player right into short-season A ball is something else," Lieppman said. "He's got some of the intangibles that a high pick really needs. He has excellent hands and a good bat. He has a lot going for him. It's just a matter of refining his skills right now."

D'Amico wasn't signed to play any particular position. He played shortstop, pitched, and played third base so well in high school that the Whitecaps considered him for all three spots. Since the draft, he's emerged as a shortstop, something D'Amico is a little surprised about.

"Shortstop is what I do best," D'Amico said. "But because I'm so tall and baseball tends to want smaller, quicker, players at this position, it does surprise me that they've kept me here."

Whitecaps manager Jim Colborn sees it differently. "Well, Cal Ripken is tall, and so is Don Kessinger," Colborn said. "He's a young kid with a lot of baseball tools. His swing reminds me of Robin Yount's swing. He has a good arm and good hands."

Now with his career directed toward the infield instead of the hardwood, D'Amico won't try basketball after he retires from baseball. "There's no way I'll be able to play basketball again," said a grinning D'Amico. "Jordan's the only guy who can pull off something like that."

Keith Lieppman, Director of Player Development

No matter how quick he throws to second, or how far he hits the ball, Whitecaps catcher Willie Morales knows who has a stronger effect on his future.

"From what I've seen so far, I think he has all of the influence in the world," said Morales about Keith Lieppman, director of player development. "You want to make him happy.

He's not the kind of guy you want to piss off. You also don't want to go so far as to play to please him. You don't want to think to yourself, 'Lieppman's in the stands, so I better do good.'"

For three seasons, Lieppman has been a vital cog in the Oakland Athletics organization. He oversees all minor league managers, coaches, and players. During the spring and well after the teams break camp, all of the managers are to report to Lieppman every day with progress on each player.

He's also responsible for player contracts, making trades, and moving players and coaches to different levels. Lieppman has been involved with the A's as a player and a minor league manager since 1971.

As a player, Lieppman was a career minor leaguer. He was drafted as a third baseman by the A's in 1971. By 1973 Lieppman had advanced to Class AAA, remaining there until he retired as a player.

All during his playing tenure, Lieppman's name would always surface as the infielder that the A's would call up for late season help. But he never got the call. "I was always a step away from that dream," said Lieppman, during a brief break amidst the heat at Scottsdale Community College. "I never really lost that dream, and I always pursued it."

Lieppman's dream eventually led him to ten years as a manager in the A's minor league system. After this stint, his vision was redirected. "At one time I thought I wanted to be a first base or third base coach on the major league level," Lieppman said. "But the more I got into it, the more I realized that I enjoyed working with minor league players. I think the players know where I'm coming from."

Willie Morales said Lieppman's past experience proves that he knows what he's talking about. "His biggest thing is that he wants us to play hard at all times," said Morales, who hit .260 with the Class A Southern Oregon A's last year. "He just wants to see a bunch of hustling ball players."

Lieppman added, "I never made it to the big leagues, but I know the mistakes I made to prevent me from getting there. I can teach (minor league) players the procedures and help them get there."

The Season Begins

In early April, West Michigan's new baseball team broke camp in Arizona and departed for Chicago. From there the Whitecaps headed by bus for their road opener against the South

The first of many sellout crowds packs Old Kent Park.
Courtesy the *Grand Rapids Press*.

Bend Silver Hawks. They lost two of three in the opening series to the Silver Hawks, who are affiliated with the Chicago White Sox.

The hunger for baseball in West Michigan was displayed when three chartered buses arrived at Coveleski Stadium. Hours before the fans arrived, the players were greeted with a media frenzy from Grand Rapids and Kalamazoo. This was nothing compared to what would be in store three days later when the Whitecaps opened at home.

Home Opener

Minutes before the gates of Old Kent Park were scheduled to open and ring in opening day, Whitecaps general manager Scott Lane looked out of the window of his office, seething with disappointment. Rain continued to fall, threatening the Whitecaps' home opener against the Burlington Bees and forcing the front office to worry and scurry with a contingency plan.

The Whitecaps sent a memo to the media announcing that if the home opener was rained out, the Whitecaps would consider the following game the opener and fans with opening day tickets could use their tickets for that day. However, those with tickets for the following day would have to exchange them for any other game, based on availability.

This wasn't the type of start that president Lew Chamberlin and owner Dennis Baxter had in mind. Neither did Lane. "It had rained all morning, and things didn't look good for us," Lane said about that drizzly day. "Lew, Dennis, and I had decided that if the game was a rainout that we would honor opening day tickets the following day. We felt that we had an obligation to everyone who stood in line for tickets in March. But we were getting heat about our plan from the media and from the fans who held tickets for the following day."

While Lane continued to gaze out his window, Jay Lowe, the producer of Grand Rapids' WZZM-TV, stood in Lane's office doorway with some news. Lowe's meteorologist assured that the rain would subside enough to play. "I got on the telephone and told Lew 'let's play,'" Lane said. "Just as I said that, the rain eased up, and we opened the gates an hour before game time. Everything worked out. I was especially happy for the crowd that stood in line for opening day tickets."

♦ ♦ ♦

So were the fans. Especially Jeff Barton, who had snuggled into position nineteen hours before the doors opened at West Michigan's temporary office in downtown Grand Rapids. On March 5, at 3:25 P.M., Barton propped up his tent, spread out his sleeping bag, turned on his radio, and began his wait. "I'm doing this for the historical significance," Barton said late that winter evening. "There'll be only one grand opening day."

The thirty-two-year-old Barton planned in advance for this venture. He had purchased the tent for his ten-year-old son, but didn't think he'd be the one to break it in. "We put the tent up in the house for practice," Barton said. By 11 P.M. twenty-eight more fans were lined up behind Barton, ready to brave the chill for opening day tickets that wouldn't go on sale until 10 A.M. Saturday. During the night and into the wee hours of the morning, the line continued to swell. Fans began to chant, and they also started the first wave of the season.

John Barton, the Whitecaps' first fan, camps out for opening day tickets. Courtesy the *Grand Rapids Press*.

Calvin College seniors Joe Vaadrager and Joel Bulkema set the pace for the crowd. "I've done this before for Chicago Bulls and Bears games," said Bulkema, a Chicago native. "This was easier than Chicago. The people here cooperated. Joe was the life of the party." Vaadrager, of Grand Rapids, added, "We got the wave going, and we played cards all night. Some people were sleeping when I arrived at midnight, so I woke them up."

When the sun began to rise early Saturday morning, the crowd that had grown to nearly one thousand also rose. The Whitecaps served pizza, hot dogs, and soda for an early breakfast, and fans were entertained by a Dixieland band. At one point, owner Dennis Baxter couldn't hold back his elation at the community's response, and he led the crowd in singing "Take Me Out to the Ballgame."

After waiting all night, Jeff Barton finally purchased his

eight tickets. "It was worth standing in line for," he said with relief. "Look at all of the people out here, and look at all of the people who got turned away. I feel sorry for them, but I had to sacrifice, and I had a good time."

◆ ◆ ◆

Barton's good times continued as he and 6,209 fans witnessed the opening of Old Kent Park. The game was televised live, and media from all over the state of Michigan packed the press box. Despite the soggy conditions, nothing could dampen the excitement and the glamour of the first professional baseball game in Grand Rapids since 1951. The players were as excited as the fans. "I thought it was unbelievable," said pitcher Matt

Victorious Whitecaps salute the crowd after downing Burlington in the home opener. Courtesy the *Grand Rapids Press*.

Walsh on his first look at Old Kent Park. "I never expected anything like this."

Neither did the fans who watched that dramatic first game. Ticket scalpers sold $5 tickets for $20 before game time. A Dixieland band greeted fans who lined up hours in advance. Once inside, fans looked around in amazement at the 5,700 seat, $6 million ball park, and then dashed for their seats.

When mist began to hover over Old Kent Park, it sounded a red alert in the memories of West Michigan pitcher Chris Michalak and catcher Willie Morales. "We were on the bench talking about games in the Cape Cod League," said Michalak, about a summer collegiate baseball league based in Massachusetts. "That's where the fog comes in, and games will be called after five innings. So I said, "Let's get some runs, and if the rain comes we'll be ahead.'"

Down by a run and fueled on urgency, Morales stepped to the plate and smacked a two-run fourth-inning homer to spark a three-run inning and a 5-2 home opener win over the Burlington Bees. "I knew it was gone," said Michalak, who got the win. "When you see a swing like that, nice and easy, that's when a ball just takes off."

Morales, who picked up two hits in the game, said he ranks the smash high on his career highlight list. "It's right up there, because if you do something good in front of a new crowd, hopefully it'll stick as a positive in their minds." At the end of the season the fans would vote him the most popular player, in part because of his dramatic introduction this day. "Plus, any time you can help your team win a ball game, that's also something you'll remember for along time," Morales said.

This game will also be remembered for a spectacular catch made by left fielder Tony Banks. The catch, however, was ruled a no-catch by the field umpire.

After the Whitecaps had taken a 3-1 lead following

Morales' homer, Burlington got two consecutive singles in the top of the fifth. Both runners moved to second and third on a sacrifice bunt. The Bees' Juan Batista then drilled a high fly ball to left field.

"When it was hit, I went back and looked up," Banks said. "As I looked up, I thought to myself how foggy it was. When I looked down at the warning track I lost the ball for a moment. When I re-focused on it again, I lost my balance and fell back and caught it, but the umpire didn't think so."

Whitecaps manager Jim Colborn immediately had a briefing with the umpire. "He caught it, period," Colborn said. "The umpire couldn't see it. It's a two-man crew, it was foggy, and he has to stay in the infield. That's asking a lot. I can see how you might not see that. It was an unorthodox catch, but he caught it. Thank goodness it didn't affect the game."

Despite the soggy conditions, Banks said the fan support spiced the game. "I honestly didn't believe we'd play tonight," he said. "I guess it was just in the cards for us to open. It was fun because the fans were very supportive. With the weather conditions, I thought they'd be dead. They're definitely ready for a squad."

Rain did fall momentarily in the fourth and fifth innings, but neither inclement weather nor hour-long traffic delays on U.S. 131 and West River Drive could dampen the enthusiasm of a Whitecaps crowd that cheered from the first pitch through the postgame fireworks.

The Whitecaps expected plenty of enthusiasm, but no one imagined anything quite like this. Pitcher Zack Sawyer was so impressed that he jokingly said: "Forget playing for the Oakland A's. I want to stay in Grand Rapids."

A Long Time Coming

The last pro baseball team in Grand Rapids was the Grand Rapids Chicks of the All-American Girls Professional Baseball League that disbanded after the 1954 season. The last men's pro team was the Grand Rapids Jets of the Central League. Thirty-six teams played minor league baseball in Grand Rapids from 1883 to 1954 under names like the Woodworkers, Grads, Billbobs, Boers, Cabinetmakers, Black Sox, Furnituremakers, Champs, Blackbirds, and Rustlers.

But the most popular team was the Chicks. Their league was the brainchild of Chicago Cubs owner Peter K. Wrigley. The league initially began as an alternate plan to provide baseball in Chicago in case the 1944 major league season was canceled by World War II. The Chicks came to Grand Rapids in 1945 and stayed for ten years, playing to a full house at South Field where they drew an average of one hundred thousand fans a season. They even outdrew their male counterparts the Jets, who played at Bigelow Field.

Throughout the years, several local players went on to play in the major leagues, including Benny McCoy, Mickey Stanley, Dave Rozema, Jon Vander Wal, Brent Gates, and Wally Pipp. Pipp holds the distinction of being the first baseman replaced by Lou Gehrig, who went on to become a legendary star for the New York Yankees.

Midwest League

Teams in Illinois, Michigan, Indiana, Iowa, and Wisconsin made up the Midwest League in 1994. The league began in 1949 as the Mississippi-Ohio Valley League, and when league boundaries were reduced to the states of Iowa, Illinois, and Indiana at one point in the 1960s, it was called the Three-I League. In 1994 the league consisted of a Southern Division and Northern Division, with teams playing a 140-game schedule. The season was split into a first and a second half.

A team had two chances to make the playoffs or win the division outright. If a team won more games than the other teams in its division in the first seventy games of the season, then that team would make the playoffs. If a different team won the most games in the second half, then that team would win the division for that half and the two teams would meet in the playoffs. If the same team won each half, then the team that finished in second for the entire season would qualify for the playoffs.

The Northern Division was made up of West Michigan, Rockford (Illinois), Beloit (Wisconsin), Appleton (Wisconsin), South Bend (Indiana), Kane County (Illinois), and Fort Wayne (Indiana). The Southern Division consisted of Cedar Rapids (Iowa), Springfield (Illinois), Peoria (Illinois), Madison (Wisconsin), Quad City (Iowa), Clinton (Iowa), and Burlington (Iowa).

In 1987, George Spelius became the seventh president of the Midwest League. Spelius had been the director of the Beloit Brewers from 1982-84 and then served as vice president of the Central Division in 1986 (when the league had three divisions). That same year league president Bill Walters died, and the three division presidents cooperated to run the league in the interim before team owners elected Spelius to succeed Walters.

Housing

When it came to finding housing for the summer, the most fortunate player was catcher Randy Ortega. While none of the opening day Whitecaps players were from Michigan, Ortega was the only player who had ever been to Grand Rapids.

In 1991, Ortega played on the Little Caesar baseball team that finished seventh in the NABC World Series. That summer the Stockton, California, native lived with Grand Rapids Ottawa Hills High School star Harry Berrios, who now plays in the Baltimore Orioles organization.

Ortega said he came to Grand Rapids because he learned that the team needed a catcher. He also wanted a chance to play summer baseball. "I really enjoyed my two months here," Ortega said. "The Berrios family was really nice, and I couldn't wait to get here so I could look up some friends I had made."

Like most of the players, Ortega also had the task of finding housing while in West Michigan for the summer. Luckily, the Berrios family was willing to take him in again. "It makes me feel good that I can live with them," Ortega said. "I've already had a great experience living here before. I'm sure it'll only be better this time around."

Several players decided to get apartments together, but most found life better moving in with a family. The families also enjoyed their new lives created by the players. But Brenda Karsies didn't have the slightest idea of how much her involvement in the West Michigan Whitecaps Keep-A-'Cap program would change her life.

For the past five years, Brenda and her husband, Ron, have opened their home to exchange students from all over the world. For ten months out of the year, the Karsies' home becomes a junior United Nations. So she figured providing a home for a Whitecaps baseball player wouldn't be any different from what she'd done in the past.

This time she was wrong. "I never thought it would be this way," Brenda said. "I figured this would be something I'd enjoy, but I didn't think something like this would happen."

She was referring to what happened when the Karsies' three new tenants, Dominican Republic natives Jose Guillen, Vinny Francisco, and Juan Dilone, were heading out of the door for the Whitecaps' first road trip in early April. The team would be away for eight days, and Brenda and her two children, Jordon, six, and Kelli Jo, eight, couldn't control their emotions. "They all came over and gave me and the children a big hug," Brenda said. "When they left, the kids and I were crying. I had to call up one of my girlfriends to cheer me up."

Flowing tears certainly wasn't what Whitecaps general manager Scott Lane or vice president Lew Chamberlin had in mind when they instituted this program. It was created by the Whitecaps' front office for individuals or families interested in "adopting" a player, by offering housing and the comforts of home from mid-April to early September.

"We had the same program in Kane County," said Lane, who had previously been with that minor league club. "We believed it would work well here because of the Little Caesars baseball team that has a similar plan."

Lane also said that living with a family has other advantages for the players. "We believe something like this is a plus because minor league ball players don't make a lot of money," Lane said. "This is also something that gets them directly involved with the community."

Class A players average one thousand dollars per month during the five-month season. Players are responsible for their own housing arrangements and must provide their own meals. Players do receive fifteen dollars per day on the road. Taking advantage of this type of program was beneficial for players living on a tight budget.

Dick and Julie Clebeck are also veterans of the Little Caesars' plan of placing players with local families for the summer. That's why they welcomed the addition of pitchers Ryan Whitaker and Derek Manning. "We've been fortunate to have some good kids from Little Caesars stay here in the past," said Julie. "And we really enjoy Ryan and Derek. Our three daughters think of them as their big brothers."

The Whitecaps' plan went into motion in January with a press release asking interested families to write a letter telling why they would want to host a player. The Karsies read the story in the *Grand Rapids Press* and decided to go into action. Their letter stated how they've shared their home in the past and how their church activities could be attractive.

About twenty-three of these letters were approved. They were then sent to spring training in Scottsdale, where the players were preparing for the upcoming season. The players could read the letters and call a family to set up some living arrangements once arriving in Grand Rapids. But the Karsies never got a call. "I came home every day and turned on my answering machine, but there was never a message from a player," Brenda said. "I was getting disappointed."

After the players arrived in Grand Rapids the second week of April, the Whitecaps set up an informal open house at Old Kent Park for those players and families who were still looking for a connection. Once the introductions were made, and after some players decided on other families, the Karsies thought they were out in the cold again, until . . .

"We were ready to leave, and then the Whitecaps management asked if there was anyone willing to host three players," Brenda said. "I just looked at Ron, and I knew we had the room. After Dilone talked to us and two other interested families, we left the stadium not knowing if we were ever going to get a player." Later that evening, Dilone, Guillen, and Francisco came by the Karsies' house, looked around for five minutes, and then asked where to put their bags.

After that, the Karsies household was never quite the same. "They kicked me out of my kitchen," said Brenda, who owns a vending machine company. "They won't let me do anything. Jose always does the cooking. We call him Chef Jose. He makes great rice dishes. One day I tried to go into the dishwasher and they told me to go do something else, as they took over and cleaned the kitchen. Jose also does the other guys' laundry."

And while Brenda tried to help around her own house, the trio would be in the process of entertaining her children. The guys would either be playing baseball with Jordon or bouncing on a trampoline with Kelli Jo. The Karsies also included the Dominicans in their church recreation activities. "We taught them how to play spoons," Brenda said. "We'll go out for pizza, and we'll go bowling. We always try to go out and do fun stuff as a family."

There wasn't much of a language barrier because Dilone speaks excellent English, Francisco does fairly well, and Guillen is coming along. But because of the previous Latin American exchange students, Brenda said communicating wasn't a problem. "We don't speak Spanish, but we're all very used to trying to decipher things because of our exchange students," Brenda said. "And if you're talking to Jose and you ask if he understands and he says yes, we figure he doesn't understand."

As everyone became closer, Ron noticed a change in his wife. "She's never been a big baseball fan," he said. "That may have changed since the Whitecaps have been living with us." When the team was in town, the Karsies were at the ball park. When the team was on the road, the family tuned in the game on radio. "We don't miss a game," Brenda said. "They're not Whitecaps players. They're my kids."

Brenda knew all good things had to come to an end. She didn't look forward to the end of the season. "I'm going to miss them big time. They're a huge part of our lives right now, and I know I'll be a wreck when they leave."

Take Me Out to the Ballgame

The freshly groomed field immediately grabbed the attention of every first-time visitor to Old Kent Park. From there, the eyes would scan the outfield wall, where the billboard advertisements mesh together like a psychedelic maze.

Packs of children frolicked up and down the grassy slopes, the lawn seating area that stretches behind the third and first base foul lines. Once the aroma of hot dogs, popcorn, and pork chop sandwiches filled the air, fans couldn't help but line up at the concession stands.

As the day evolved into evening, it was time for baseball to begin, accompanied by a continuous subplot of characters and events that shed a ray of sunshine on every fan that entered Old Kent Park.

High-fiving, Whitecap-clapping, fan-loving "Hurricane" Henry Gendron became a huge part of the magic that embraced West Michigan home games. Gendron, an employee of Consumers Power, was the most popular usher at the park. Hurricane Henry, who got his nickname from Whitecaps announcer Rick Berkey, did more than help fans find their seats. Henry came into his own during Whitecaps rallies. This is when the barrel-shaped Henry mounted his stage atop the

Michael Zelenka and Theresa Agius of Saugatuck Township enjoy the pork chop sandwich, a favorite at Old Kent Park.
Courtesy the *Grand Rapids Press*.

Whitecaps dugout to stomp his feet, clap his hands, and fire up the crowd with chants of "Let's go, let's go." Children flocked to Henry like a pied piper. He signed more autographs than any non-player at the park, with the exception of team mascot "Crash the River Rascal."

The most anticipated between-innings stunt took place early in the game when Crash would race around the bases against an eager child. The first one home would win a prize. Without fail, Crash, who resembles a cross between a muskrat and a gopher, would take the lead heading for home. But just before Crash could cash in his winnings, a sudden fall or interference by manager Jim Colborn or the visiting catcher would prevent the rodent from claiming victory.

The bat races were also a hot slapstick event between

innings. Two exuberant fans would be chosen to compete in a race to second base from the on-deck circle. Fan one would head to second by way of third base, while fan two took the usual route past first. Simply running the bases would have been easy enough, but a twist was added. First each participant had to stand a bat on its head, put his or her forehead on the end of the bat, and circle the bat several times. Then the two would be signalled to run to second base. That's when the fun would begin. The woozy contestants would stagger sideways, collide with a player, or plummet to the ground as the crowd roared in laughter.

Yet another episode took place after the seventh-inning stretch. The chicken dance craze that swept through major and minor league parks across the country couldn't pass up Old Kent Park. "Hurricane" Henry, Crash, and Whitecaps staff members would line up fans on the roof of each dugout, and this chorus line would persuade the remaining fans in the park to join in. The music blared and the dance began, with fans flapping their arms, doing a semi-twist to a squat, and clapping their hands.

Amid this circus atmosphere, the fans also watched a baseball game.

Controversy

Whitecaps fans were introduced to controversy early in the season. In a mid-April home game, it was the hit heard around West Michigan, and it was seen only by Rockford's Carlos Mendez and home plate umpire Steve Rackley.

A two-run seventh-inning homer by Mendez helped give the Royals a 7-4 victory over West Michigan on a Sunday afternoon at Old Kent Park. The loss split the two-game series, as the Whitecaps and Royals tied for second place in the North Division of the Midwest League with 5-4 records.

The Whitecaps came back from a 4-1 deficit, sparked by a two-run home run by Juan Dilone in the fifth. Dilone's shot made it 4-3. In the seventh, with Rockford's Sal Fasano on first, Mendez stepped to the plate, setting up the most highly-disputed call at Old Kent Park since Whitecaps Tony Banks' catch on opening night was ruled a hit.

As Fasano ran with the pitch, Mendez hit a high swerving ball to right field that was hooking right before it landed over the fence in foul territory. After a ten-second pause, Rackley shot his arm to his left signaling fair ball. It gave Mendez a home run and the Royals a 6-3 lead.

After the signal, Whitecaps manager Jim Colborn sprinted to the home plate umpire on a wave of boos from the crowd of 5,960. After he left the field, kicking the right foul line in disgust, the ball in question sailed back onto the field amidst a cheer.

The ball was thrown back by Lenny Padilla, a sophomore at Grand Rapids Community College. "I was behind the fence on those dirt mounds," Padilla said. "It bounced and I caught it on the rebound. I assumed that it was foul, so I put my hands up cheering. When it was ruled a home run, I thought that was crazy. I decided to throw it back."

But Mendez had a different view. "It just made it," he said, while his teammates in the Rockford locker room chanted, "Foul ball, foul ball." "I hit the ball good. When I rounded first base, I kept running when I saw the umpire call it fair."

Royals manager John Mizerock also saw Mendez' hit with the same prescription glasses. "Of course it was a home run.

The umpire called it a home run," said a half grinning Mizerock. "But I really couldn't tell by how much."

Whitecaps outfielder David Keel, who stood near the line watching the flight of the ball, said he saw by how much the ball was foul. "I was just shocked when he called it a home run," Keel said. "I was right there on the line, and it was foul. Of course, the guy that hit it would think it was fair. If I would've hit one that was questionable like that, I would try to convince myself that it was a legitimate home run too."

Whitecaps pitcher Tim Kubinski was also in a state of confusion with the call. Thinking it was foul, he went to the umpire to retrieve another ball. As he approached him, Kubinski saw the signal and was stunned. "I asked him what he was doing. (Rackley) said he lost it for a moment and picked it up behind the foul pole, like it curved around.

"When the ball was thrown back, I probably would've laughed if the homer wasn't on me. I like people agreeing with me, especially since it wasn't a fair ball."

Manager Jim Colborn wouldn't repeat exactly what he said to the umpire, but he knows there wasn't much he could do after the call. "What can I say," Colborn said. "There's no recourse. That ball went over the sign on the right side of the foul pole."

◆ ◆ ◆

More controversy and the first major injury awaited the Whitecaps on their next road trip to Springfield and Cedar Rapids.

Shortstop Jeff D'Amico became the first West Michigan casualty when he damaged his anterior cruciate ligament on April 20 in Springfield, when he caught his spikes in the dirt while running the bases. D'Amico, who was chosen by the Oakland Athletics in the second round of the 1993 draft, missed the rest of the season. On April 23 the Whitecaps called up Marcel Galligani from the extended spring program for D'Amico's spot on the roster.

Later D'Amico underwent surgery performed by Dr. Lewis Yokum at the Jobe Clinic in Inglewood, California. "You get an empty feeling when something like this happens. It feels like someone punched me in the stomach. But the only thing I can do is make a comeback," D'Amico said.

After surgery, D'Amico began rehabilitation of his left knee. Doctors told him it would take six to nine months of rehab for a full recovery. But D'Amico was ready for the new challenge. "I'll focus on rehab the same way I do anything else," said D'Amico, who resides in Redmond, Washington. "I'm young, and I'll have time. But it's weird being home because it feels like the offseason."

◆ ◆ ◆

During the "inning from hell" in a Sunday afternoon game at Cedar Rapids, West Michigan pitcher Tim Bojan made a choice — if you can't beat 'em, bean 'em.

Bojan entered the sixth inning with a two-run lead over the Kernels. By the time he was replaced in that same inning, Cedar Rapids had scored six runs. The Kernels ran away with a 15-3 victory before 1,417 fans at Veterans Memorial Stadium. It was the Whitecaps' fourth consecutive defeat, as they dropped to 7-8 in the Northern Division. The Kernels went to 6-7 in the Southern Division.

That one inning took thirty-eight minutes to complete. It was highlighted by what might have turned into a brawl when Bojan hit two consecutive batters.

The incident especially didn't sit well with Derrin Doty. He was the second Kernel to get nailed. "It looked like he was trying to hit me," Doty said. "We had a big inning, and a couple of cheap hits. I think he was frustrated."

First, Tony Moeder was popped and was given first base. Then Doty was hit in the back on the first pitch, and he had to be restrained by Whitecaps catcher Randy Ortega. "He just woke up a sleeping dog," said Doty about his team's three-game winning streak. "He just motivated us even more."

The beaning may have motivated Doty, but it also eased Bojan's pain. "They were hitting me all over the place," said an 0-1 Bojan. I didn't want to hit the second guy (Doty). I was just trying to come in on him. But I meant to hit the first guy (Moeder)." By hitting Moeder, Bojan said he was able to relieve some stress.

"When I came into the locker room after the game I asked, 'Am I like Derek Manning?'" said Bojan, about Manning who gave up six runs on seven hits in a nightmarish inning in South Bend. "Now I know how he felt. But I can't worry about this, because it's just a game. I'll just have to work harder at it."

Early signs that the Whitecaps might halt their losing streak occurred when Mark Moore's solo shot in the second inning gave them a 1-0 lead. The Whitecaps added more runs in the fourth. A solo homer by newcomer Marcel Galligani and Moore's second homer made the lead 3-1.

Then came that crucial inning with Bojan on the mound, replacing Ryan Whitaker. A single and two walks loaded the bases with one out. A three-run triple gave the Kernels a one-run lead. A walk and a double scored two more runs, and Cedar Rapids had a 6-3 edge.

That was when Bojan hit the next two batters. After a single made it 7-3, Whitecaps manager Jim Colborn couldn't stand it anymore, and he pulled Bojan for reliever William Urbina.

Bojan left the field in a huff. He took a seat at the end

of the bench, away from his teammates. "I can only take this like any other day," Bojan said. "Sure, I'm disappointed about the results, but I can't sit and dwell on it. I have to laugh at it. It'll kill you if you let it eat at you."

Bojan stopped laughing after he was fined twenty-five dollars by league president George Spelius. Someone faxed a newspaper article to Spelius in which Bojan was quoted as saying he had hit the player (Moeder) on purpose.

◆ ◆ ◆

Outfielder Jason McDonald should have had an indication of what the trip to Iowa was going to be like. When the team arrived at their hotel in Cedar Rapids, McDonald checked in and went to the room that was written on his key. As he put the key in the door, he got a surprise. "I kept trying the key and twisting the knob but it wouldn't open," McDonald said. "Then I heard someone yell from within that I had the wrong room. If it would've opened I could've been shot or something. I'm glad the key didn't work."

First Addition

While lounging poolside in the Scottsdale heat, Marcel Galligani received a highly anticipated, but yet an unexpected message.

"I got a call from my manager," said Galligani, in his thick New York accent. "I didn't think much of it, because I thought he wanted to talk about something we'd already discussed earlier that day. My roommate told me that I'd better call, because it could mean that I was out of here."

Galligani was ready to leave the extended spring training program. This is for players who play a short season that begins in June. Oakland's short season teams are Southern Oregon and Scottsdale. Galligani was headed for Southern Oregon until he returned the telephone call.

"I was ready to get out of that heat," said Galligani, about the 100-plus temperatures in Arizona. "I couldn't take it anymore."

Galligani had to take a flight to Cedar Rapids from Arizona, and he arrived at Veterans Memorial Stadium in Cedar Rapids in the first inning. He was added to the twenty-five-man roster because of the season-ending knee injury suffered by shortstop Jeff D'Amico in Springfield.

Galligani himself was no stranger to injury. After being drafted by the Oakland Athletics out of Iona College in 1992, the native of Mamaroneck, New York, hadn't had much luck. "My first year I sprained ligaments in my thumb, so I had to stay a year in extended season," Galligani said. "This year I came into spring training with an ear infection. I've had it for about three months. It's better. I'm at about 90 percent."

The addition of Galligani brought experience to several positions. Drafted as a shortstop, Galligani was an outfielder for Iona. This year he played several positions for the Whitecaps. "I've brought five different gloves with me," said Galligani, who plays every position except catcher. "I'll play wherever I'm needed."

Galligani quickly made his presence known, hitting a home run in his first start and second at-bat as a Whitecap.

◆ ◆ ◆

43

After eight days on their first long road trip, the Whitecaps were eager to return to Old Kent Park — except for Vinny Francisco.

Francisco, Scott Baldwin, and Tim Bojan were the only married Whitecaps players, and Cedar Rapids is the home of Francisco's wife, Alexandra. They met at a Burger King last year when Vinny visited Cedar Rapids as a player for Madison. After a month, the couple "had it their way" and were married in Madison that August. Now they were expecting their first child in June.

Alexandra, who graduated from high school in May, circled the Whitecaps' trip to Cedar Rapids on her calendar. "I didn't sleep for two days until he got here," Alexandra said.

Vinny Francisco lays down a bunt.   Courtesy the *Grand Rapids Press.*

"That's how excited I was. Vinny and I only see each other about once a month. It's very hard. You have to be so committed. You have to have that true love if you want it to last. But I don't like it. I do get frustrated some times."

After the wedding, Alexandra traveled back to the Dominican Republic with Vinny and stayed there until January. She said she enjoyed her visit with her in-laws. Despite her background, the language was a small problem. "I was born in South America," said Alexandra, brushing her long black hair away from her eyes. "I was adopted by my American family and brought here when I was nine years old. My Spanish isn't great, but Vinny is teaching me, and I'm helping him with English."

Because of the pregnancy, Alexandra remained in Cedar Rapids with her family, despite the heartache it caused. "I see her every month," Francisco said. "I'd like to see her more often, but she can't travel much now because of the pregnancy. But after she has the baby, she'll move in with me in Grand Rapids."

The baby decided to arrive on June 9 while the Whitecaps were playing at Fort Wayne. Vinny arrived at the hospital after Vinny Jr. was born, and received some unpleasant news. Vinny Jr. did not arrive without complications. After a difficult labor, doctors performed a Cesarean section. The baby developed a condition called meconium stool aspiration and began bleeding from the lungs shortly after the C-section, but doctors were able to stabilize him. Meconium stool aspiration is a condition which develops during long, stressful labors and usually does not carry long-term effects. Infants with the condition typically remain hospitalized for two to three days for observation before being released. Vinny Jr. remained in the hospital for a month.

Vinny Sr. didn't return to Old Kent Park for several days. "I was told that if they didn't take him to another hospital to a specialist in ten more minutes, he would've died," said Francisco. "They took him from Cedar Rapids to a hospital in Iowa City by helicopter. I missed him when I left the hospital."

Football's Loss

Jason McDonald was glad things worked out for him in baseball despite a mishap that ended another possible career. As a wide receiver for the University of Houston in 1992, one yard prevented McDonald from scoring his only major collegiate touchdown. Just one yard separated the Whitecaps second baseman from a probable pro football career, but that one yard helped propel his quest into major league baseball.

"In the third quarter, quarterback Jimmy Klinger called an audible to my side," explained McDonald, about the fourth game of the 1992 season against Southwestern Louisiana. "I was open, and he hit me with a pass on the line. I took off down field for forty-eight yards, and then I was hit right on the one-yard line. Both of my knees hit right on the turf. I popped up right away, and I felt my knee hurting. At the end of that quarter I couldn't walk."

McDonald strained the posterior cruciate ligament (PCL) in his left knee. Surgery wasn't needed, but McDonald could have used a boost in confidence. "I felt down on my luck," said the Elk Grove, California, native. "I didn't know what was going to happen. I was a long way from home. I was just getting acclimated to Houston, and then I got hurt. All I could

Jason McDonald stretches for the force-out at second.
Courtesy the *Grand Rapids Press.*

do was rehab every day. It didn't seem like my knee was getting any better."

McDonald's football career ended before it could really begin on the Division I level. Houston had recruited McDonald out of Sacramento City College, where he finished a splendid season by making sixty-five catches for 980 yards and thirteen touchdowns. Former Cougar coach John Jenkins, now an assistant with the Winnipeg Blue Bombers of the Canadian Football League, wanted McDonald immediately after watching him in action.

"I was attracted to his quickness and his cutting ability," Jenkins said. "The fact that he was small (five-foot-eight) didn't bother me, because I went for speed instead of size. To this day, he could be a factor as a return specialist for a pro football team, but I also know he's a solid baseball player."

After his fate in football was decided, McDonald began to rehab and concentrate on his other scholarship sport. When the baseball season began on February 1, he still had some knee pain. Cougar manager Bragg Stockton insisted that McDonald wear a knee brace, although the player found it to be uncomfortable.

McDonald finally got rid of the brace in the first game, when it was mangled as he slid into third base. "They had to order a new one," said McDonald, who was pleased at the time. "So I started to use this little plastic brace that the trainer put together with wraps. I liked this one much better because it gave my knee more mobility. My knee began to heal. Later that year I got rid of the brace."

McDonald played in forty-four of fifty-five games during the Cougars 1992-93 season, hitting .272 and stealing twenty bases in twenty-eight attempts. He was drafted by the Oakland Athletics in the fourth round of the June 1993 free agent draft.

"I expected to get drafted, but not as high as I did," McDonald said. "I had a sub-par baseball season. I was thinking I had to come back for my senior year because of the season I had. I was also looking forward to playing football."

But once again, football got booted when McDonald signed with Oakland. According to his contract, he had to agree not to play football while a member of the A's organization. That decision wasn't too hard a pill to swallow.

"Baseball is my first love, and I've always wanted to play the sport," said McDonald, who led the Midwest League in steals and triples. "Getting hurt in football gave me a big scare. I've been told ever since high school that I shouldn't play football because I could get hurt. I remembered that while sitting in my my room wondering if I'd be able to play baseball again."

Still, every fall McDonald gets a certain itch. "When

football season comes around and I see all of my friends playing, it makes me wonder what if I would've kept going," McDonald said. "I do miss it a lot, especially when I watch college football on TV."

But there is one thing McDonald doesn't miss about football and wishes he could forget. On September 26, 1992, in Ann Arbor the University of Michigan defeated Houston 61-7. And that wasn't the worst of it. "I received a punt, ran about ten yards, and there was no one but me and the punter," said a grinning McDonald. "I slowed down to go out of bounds, thinking the punter wouldn't hit me. He just leveled me, and my feet went straight up in the air. It seemed like the whole Michigan crowd was just laughing at me. My teammates even let me have it."

Back on the Road

After a six-game home stand, West Michigan returned to the road. The first stop was against the Beloit Brewers for two games.

That's where pitcher Bob Bennett received a surprise. "While sitting on the bench during the game, (manager) Jim Colborn smiles and says that he has a secret," Bennett said. "I had no idea what he was talking about. I found out when we went into the locker room."

Bennett was moved to the Modesto (California) A's, a higher level Class A team in the organization. Pitcher Jason Rajotte, who was in the extended spring training program in

Scottsdale, replaced Bennett. Room was made for Bennett in Modesto when the A's number one choice from 1993, John Wasdin, was bumped up to Huntsville, Alabama (Class AA).

Colborn hated to see the Dartmouth graduate go. "I'm happy for him," Colborn said. "He's one of the finest young men who I've run into in baseball. As a pitcher, he has good poise and a good fastball. And he has good command."

The decision to move Bennett involved the collaboration of Colborn, Whitecaps pitching coach Gil Patterson, director of player development Keith Lieppman, and minor league pitching instructor Bob Cluck. "They (Modesto) needed a pitcher, and Bennett was pitching nicely," Colborn said. "There were some other guys considered. Again, I hate to see him go."

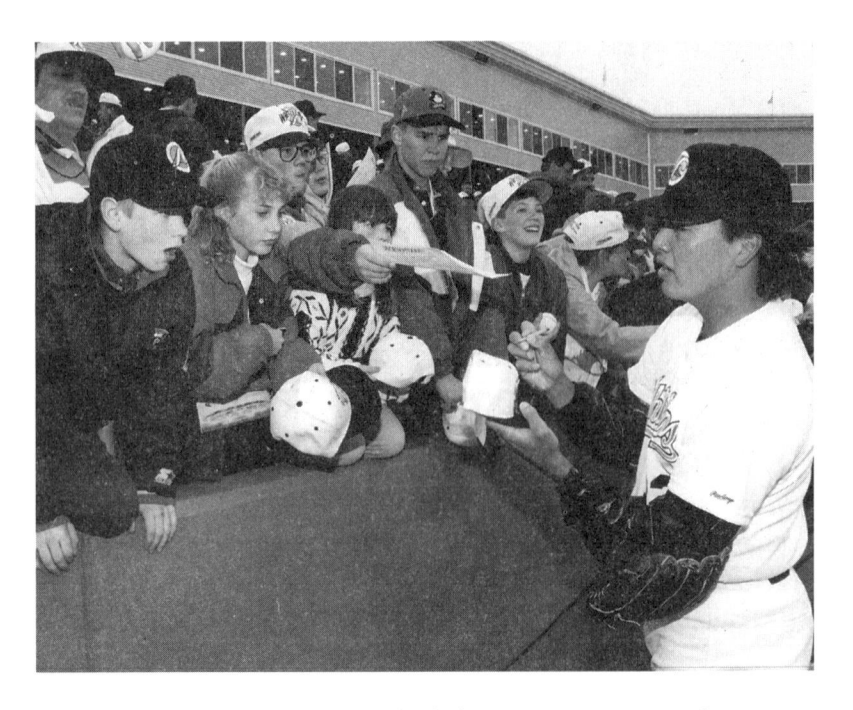

Bob Bennett signs autographs before moving up to Modesto.
Courtesy the *Grand Rapids Press*.

In twenty-four innings pitched, Bennett left with an 0-2 record and a 2.19 ERA. He struck out twenty-three batters and gave up twenty-three hits.

Bennett hoped he could continue to perform at a top level for his new team. He wasn't sure what to expect, but he did know what he would share with his new teammates. "I'll tell them that compared to Grand Rapids, Modesto is a step down," Bennett said. "I'll tell them how the town embraced us and wherever you go in town you'll see Whitecaps' stuff. I'm really going to miss it."

The purpose of the minor leagues is to develop the players and for them to move up the ladder to the different levels. Sometimes things are left behind in the move, but players have to be able to regroup and be ready to make new adjustments in a new site.

A Lakota (Sioux) from Rapid City, South Dakota, Bennett began to receive national attention because of his rediscovery of his Native American culture. Before games he would perform rituals involving tobacco and eagle feathers, rituals that his ancestors performed before going on a buffalo hunt. Bennett began to grow a hair braid like the Lakota wore. He was given the name Wanbli Wanji, meaning One Eagle.

"I always carry two eagle feathers with me," Bennett said. "An old man gave them to me. In the old days when someone did something good they would present them with a feather (as an award). It was given to someone who did good in battle, or saved someone's life. This was given to me when I graduated from high school. It's a source of strength, a source of knowledge. When I need some kind of strength I pray with this."

When he was sent to Modesto, Bennett was due to speak at a Traverse City–area Native American reservation. He had hoped to inspire youth who could benefit from his experiences. ESPN 2 planned to do a story about his speech.

"A lot of people anticipated me to be there," Bennett said. "It's kind of a letdown, but what can I do? I'm at the mercy of the Oakland A's. It's sad, because I could've been an example to kids. I could've shown them that although I play baseball, I'm still able to walk in a traditional way of life like my ancestors."

He was aware that his travels would take him to other speaking engagements. He also knew his travels would possibly lead him to another family who would take him in. And just like thousands of other minor league players, Bennett knew that you must keep moving along. That's if you want to make the big time.

◆ ◆ ◆

The big time is where Beloit pitcher Kelly Wunsch went after striking out five batters in one inning two weeks prior to West Michigan's arrival. Wunsch, who pitched for Texas A & M, became the first starter in both major and minor league history to record five strikeouts in one inning. Two relief pitchers had also struck out five in one frame, the last time in 1952.

After striking out two batters, Wunsch was helped in achieving this feat when the next two batters struck out on wild pitches. Each time, the ball got away from the catcher, allowing the batter to reach base. One more strikeout ended the inning.

Wunsch was interviewed by magazines, newspapers, and radio stations from across the country. To top things off, he made Baseball's Hall of Fame in Cooperstown, New York. A photograph of Wunsch, his baseball hat, and an autographed baseball are on display at the hall.

"I guess you can say I'm a little shocked," said Wunsch, a first-round pick of the Brewers. "I was pretty obscure in college, and I've never expected anything like this. This has put me in the spotlight, and I'm enjoying every minute of it."

The spotlight became dimmer when Wunsch was demoted by the Brewers in July because of wildness.

◆ ◆ ◆

That was just the beginning of strange events that happened at Beloit's Pohlman Field in 1994. On July 5, Beloit and Madison were tied 1-1 in the top of the ninth inning. Madison's Tom McKinnon fouled a ball off the face mask of home plate umpire Jason Gibbons. Gibbons fell to the ground and blacked out. After a seven-minute delay, Gibbons remained in and finished the top of the inning. After the half inning, Gibbons was in too much pain, and he left for the clubhouse.

Base umpire Mike Fichter replaced Gibbons behind the plate, and that's when the confusion began. Midwest League president George Spelius, who attended the game, informed Beloit manager Wayne Krenchicki and Madison's Joe Cunningham that one player from each team would be used to ump the bases until the game was decided. A heated debate between Spelius and the managers ensued, and Spelius was forced to eject Madison pitcher David Carroll, who was arguing the issue from the bench.

"If I had to do it all over again, I would've done it the same way," Spelius said. "These teams are in different divisions, they weren't playing each other again this year, and the game needed to get finished. It's also in our (Midwest League) bylaws that a player from each team will be used to umpire in cases like this."

Beloit's Brad Seitzer and Madison's Hector Colon were recruited for umpiring duty. "Skip (Krenchicki) comes over and says that I'm umpiring," Seitzer said. "I told him to stop messing around. After he told me he was serious, I didn't know what to do."

That's what Cunningham thought when Seitzer made a

call in the bottom of the tenth. Seitzer called his teammate Greg Martinez safe at first on a bang-bang play. Cunningham was quoted in the *Beliot Daily News:* "Seitzer calls that guy safe at first base, and he was out by three steps. This is bull (bleep). If that's what we have to look forward to in a league president, then we better start shopping around."

That was just the type of play that Seitzer was praying against. He felt enough pressure stepping onto the field without his glove. "Right after I called him safe, I was thinking, 'Oh God!' But I thought he was safe. I asked the first and second basemen what they thought, and they agreed with me. That made me feel better."

It may have made Seitzer feel even better when Martinez didn't score. But the Brewers did end the game in the eleventh inning on a solo homer.

Losing certainly didn't make Cunningham feel any better. "He (Spelius) was worried about the (bleep)ing weather," Cunningham told the Beloit paper. "That was horse (bleep). I'm going to call my farm director. That was ridiculous."

Cunningham's comments led to a four-game suspension by Spelius. But the event did teach Seitzer a valuable lesson. "That made me really appreciate the job done by umpires," he said. "They really have a hard job. I hope I never have to ump (while in a baseball uniform) again."

◆ ◆ ◆

Beloit manager Wayne Krenchicki was honored with the distinction of being the only manager tossed out before a game even started. Late in the season, Krenchicki was ejected by umpire Mike Schuck while exchanging lineup cards at home plate with Kane County manager Lynn Jones. Krenchicki had been ejected by the same umpiring crew (Schuck and Steve Rackley) in the tenth inning of a game two weeks prior.

Krenchicki was joined in the clubhouse by two of his players who were ejected during the game.

◆　　◆　　◆

West Michigan split two games at Beloit, and then split two at Peoria. Three out of four losses in Clinton evened the Whitecaps' record at 15-15. The trip to Clinton, the longest (355 miles from Grand Rapids) of the season, was a memorable one — but a trip the team would gladly forget.

Riverview Stadium is one of the oldest parks in minor league baseball, built in 1937. The inside of the stadium has an old Yankee Stadium feel. Seventeen pillars support a roof over the seats. A picturesque view highlights center field. One hundred feet beyond the outfield wall, the *City of Clinton* riverboat sits on the Mississippi River.

The stadium is the best thing about Clinton, because the first sign of the town is the odor from the ABC plant. The stench has the strength to make a convicted criminal confess. The plant makes everything from dog food to corn extract, and the aroma hovers over the town like a rain cloud during a sunny day.

You won't find any malls in Clinton. You have to drive to Quad City for shopping. Unemployment is high because of plant closings. Because of high unemployment, the crime rate is high, as is the drug culture that has permeated the town. It had its first gang-related drive-by shooting in 1994.

Clinton is the town that time wanted to forget. It's in a time warp in the past. While the rest of the world is in the '90s, Clinton is still celebrating the end of World War I.

No one visits Clinton unless they're hiding from the law. Well, almost no one. There are the twenty-five Clinton LumberKing minor league baseball players who play here every summer. The players ranging in age from nineteen to twenty-five all admit that they are starved socially. Things can especially be tough on the three African American players on the team, living in a town of 29,200 with less than 1 percent being black.

LumberKings outfielder Benji Simonton is one of those black players. "When you think about Iowa, it's hard to imagine many black people, so you expect it," said Simonton, who set a Midwest League record by getting on base safely fourteen consecutive times during the series with the Whitecaps. "I try not to pay too much attention to it because I'm here to play ball. You also remind yourself that you're not here to stay. This is only for the summer."

"Only for the summer" is the team battle cry when those cravings for shopping malls or night clubs come to mind. That same slogan can also lead to trouble.

Last season Simonton, his teammates, and a player for the South Bend Silver Hawks went out for a night on the town after a game. Because it was a short night, the group went to a local bar similar to the one in the movie "48 Hours" starring Eddie Murphy and Nick Nolte.

On that night, a local resident believed one of the LumberKings wanted to pick up his girlfriend. Once the players realized that they couldn't change the guy's mind, or his station wagon full of friends, they got up to leave.

"We go outside, and they follow us and won't let us get into our cars," Simonton said. "Then a guy on our team makes the comment: 'What do we have to lose? We're leaving. You have to live here and suffer.'" The poor guy resented that and took a swing at the LumberKing. Then the police showed up and were able to break things up without incident.

Simonton said that for the most part, though, no one gives the players a hard time except for a few of the local young men. "They think we're here to steal their girls," Simonton said. "The guys will stare at you for no reason. When

I say hello to some of the blacks in town, they'll look at me like 'who are you?' They perceive that the black players on the team believe that we're better than them. I'm just here to do my job and not try to take anything from anyone."

❖   ❖   ❖

Simonton did such a job on the Whitecaps that outfielder Marcel Galligani and infielder Jason McDonald were forced to pitch during the series. With a white flag at half staff, Galligani was a symbol of surrender for the Whitecaps. With a half smile, the New Yorker took his position on the pitcher's mound. He was in a hole so deep that he couldn't see daylight with binoculars.

But no matter how bizarre the circumstances, Galligani craved the opportunity to relive the events. "I was juiced," he said. "I wanted to pitch. I like pitching every now and then. I'm not saying that the other positions are boring, but it (pitching) adds a little flavor to your food. I pitched all through high school, but when I went to college (Iona) I wanted to change positions because I wanted to play every day. I couldn't deal with pitching and then waiting four days to play again."

By the way things went for the Whitecaps, they all could have used a few days off. The 17-3 shelling by the Lumber-Kings was the third consecutive loss for West Michigan.

Galligani, who pitched seven innings of mop-up in the previous season in Medford, Oregon, was reunited with the mop and bucket in this game. Down by six runs in the last two innings, and because twelve pitchers had been used in the last three games, the Whitecaps staff didn't have much of a choice.

Things didn't change much with Galligani on the mound. Before he entered, the pitching rotation of Zack Sawyer and Chris Michalak had walked nine batters and struck out only two. When Galligani left the mound, he had given up eight runs, five walks, and one highlight. "After I struck that guy out, I thought I was going to cruise through the inning. Then I couldn't find the mitt," Galligani said. "I hope we're not in this position again, because we're a better team than we've showed on this road trip. We have to get back to fundamentals."

◆ ◆ ◆

Pitching coach Gil Patterson said the recent rut was frustrating because he knew his staff had better capabilities. He said there were two major things that weren't being done. "We're walking people, and we're throwing strikes, but not quality strikes," Patterson said. "We need to check on the delivery, and we need to try the mental approach, like visualization techniques and helping the pitchers with better concentration."

Patterson's job was to help his players maintain an edge which was displayed several times during the year. "We want to avoid those roller coaster outings," Patterson said. "The staff's job is to try and get those positive outings more consistently."

Despite the numbers, Sawyer didn't see much of a problem. He believed this was just a normal rhythm of the game. "Hitters go through it, and pitchers get into slumps too," Sawyer said. "There's nothing wrong with that because it happens. But I do think a lot of it is mental. I know it is with me. You have to regroup, and sometimes it's tough to do that."

Pitcher Steve Lemke, who had won his last two outings, agreed that the staff could pull through this funk. He also mentioned another contributing factor. "Things aren't going exactly our way," Lemke said, "but maybe the LumberKings are just hot."

Bus Trips

Overwhelmingly, the worst side of minor league baseball is the long bus rides and the long days on the road.

To pass the time on road trips, West Michigan players and staff have devised ways to help Father Time speed along.

One of the most popular road-trip hobbies was a game of hackey-sack. In hackey-sack the players use their feet, heads, knees, and chests to keep a small sand-filled sack from hitting the ground as they pass it to one another, much like a miniature soccer ball. Whitecaps players played this game mostly while waiting for the bus to take them back to their hotel.

Once arriving at their living arrangements, players were creative in devising ways to make the down time go faster.

Mat "Big Screen" Reese wouldn't allow a hotel to keep him cooped up. Reese enjoyed checking out the scenes of a town, to find out what was going on. "It drives me nuts sitting in my room," Reese said. "I'll play cards with the guys or I'll go to the movies."

Another player cut out of the same mode was Juan Dilone. On away trips, Dilone liked to cruise the social scene at local night clubs. "I go to clubs with my friends, sit back, and talk about the next game," Dilone said. "I also like to find out the different names of drinks from state to state."

Some players would rather spend their time in total relaxation. That was right up Vinny Francisco and Randy Ortega's alley.

Unless his wife was in town, Francisco only came out of his room to eat, take the bus to the park, or make a cameo appearance with the boys at a dance scene. While in his room, Francisco would stretch out to absorb information from the television. "I like to watch baseball games," Francisco said. "I watch them to pick up tips from the major leaguers."

Ortega used his time on the road to continue his commitment to physical fitness. Besides lifting weights, watching television, and playing cards, Ortega was a top performer in hackey-sack.

Hackey-sack and playing cards is not exactly what manager Jim Colborn liked to indulge in on the road. He was more of a contemporary man. "I can play golf during a road trip," Colborn said. "A road trip is a time for me to be alone and work out. It's also a time to meditate, which I have to do to maintain my sanity.

"I don't have time at home. At home we have to be at the park two hours earlier than on the road. There isn't anyone asking for your time on the road. The road is time for relaxation and getting my head straight. It's a chance to get in touch with my oneness."

◆ ◆ ◆

One experienced road warrior was the Whitecaps radio announcer, Rick Berkey.

Unlike Class AAA or the major leagues where traveling by plane is the norm, all other levels of baseball use the interstate. That suited Berkey just fine. "I prefer bus travel to flying," said Berkey, who was heard on WOOD-AM. "They (players) don't realize how good they've got it with the VCR, bathroom, and being able to stop to eat. You don't have those things when you're flying."

Berkey knew flying. For more than three years he did the play-by-play for the Grand Rapids Hoops, members of the Continental Basketball Association. Half of the Hoops' fifty-six games were on the road. Frequent flier miles is the CBA motto.

"When you fly, you spend so much of your time waiting

in a hotel lobby, loading your bags, going to the airport, unloading your bags, waiting for your flight, flying to your connection site, waiting for your connecting flight, unloading your bags, loading them into the van, driving to the hotel, unloading bags, and then putting them in the room," said a winded Berkey. "Here, the bus picks you up at one site and drops you off at the other."

Adjusting to bus travel was just one thing Berkey had to adapt to coming from a CBA lifestyle. Another was the different atmosphere of the two sports.

"When a team loses in the CBA, the players are in a bad mood, the coaches are in a lousy mood, and you don't want to be around any of them," said Berkey, a thirty-nine-year-old Wyoming, Michigan, native. "But when they win, they're all on a high. If you walked onto the bus here, you wouldn't know if the team won or lost. After the first road loss I expected to have to sink into my seat and keep my mouth shut. By the same token, after a win there isn't a noticeable high. With 140 games you have to keep it at an even keel."

Berkey's background in radio is dominated by basketball and football coverage. He was concerned whether the pace of baseball would throw him off his rhythm. But although he changed dancing partners, he was able to keep up with the new beat.

"One of my weaknesses as a basketball announcer is helped by the pace of baseball," Berkey said. "In basketball, I tend to make baskets in the first quarter sound like baskets in the fourth quarter. The natural pace of a baseball game keeps me from doing that. You can't get that excited by a 2-1 pitch on the outside corner in the top of the second with a 1-0 score. But I can get excited — and did — over a twenty-foot fall-away jumper three minutes into the game."

When Berkey did get excited, he could be heard in other states. When he called a home run by a Whitecap, Berkey filled the airwaves with ". . . It has a chance. . . . That dog will dance!"

"I was considering for a long time what my home run call would be," said Berkey, the father of Jacob, six, and Lindsey, nine, and the husband of Jane. "I heard through the years that the home run call was the announcer's signature. I came up with this one while driving home from church."

◆ ◆ ◆

For five months the Whitecaps left all of the driving to Ron Webster. The father of one has worked for the Indian Trails bus company for four years. When he began with Indian Trails, he immediately set out some goals.

"I want to drive a rock or country band, and I've always wanted to spend a season with a pro team," Webster said. "I've driven a pro football team before (the Tampa Bay Buccaneers from the airport to a game), and I've had Michael Jordan on my bus (when he drove the Chicago Bulls to an exhibition game). But when we were bidding for this team, I wanted it."

When Indian Trails earned the rights to drive the Whitecaps, Webster made it plain that he would be the driver. All of the drivers had a chance to bid for this opportunity, but Webster came out on top — the first bus driver in Whitecaps' history.

Webster, better known as Ronny to the players, was constantly ribbed by the players during trips. If he made a rare wrong turn in an unfamiliar city, or if the road below was a little rough, the bus driver jokes began to fly. "If they're not picking on me, I figure something is wrong," said Webster with his usual wide smile. "As long as they're harassing or picking on me, I know everything is fine."

The crown for the king heckler belonged to pitcher Matt Walsh. "I'll definitely miss Ronny," said Walsh with a grin.

"Especially the way he drives 90 mph in the left lane. I'm surprised we're not all in jail." When hard pressed, Walsh was more sincere with his affection for Webster.

Unfortunately for Webster, Indian Trails only had a one-year contract with the team. Bidding on rights for the following season was open to any bus company. Webster started his campaign early. "I told my rep that we have to have them again," he said. "I love this. All the other drivers now wish they would've had this job. It's too late now!"

Meal Money

When told of the meal money issued to major league baseball players, Marcel Galligani started to salivate. "I'd be living large," the Whitecaps outfielder said. "I'd eat steak every day. I wouldn't have to go to the ATM."

But because of the standard minor league allotment for meal money on road trips, Galligani — and even Michael Jordan — all have to survive on the road on fifteen dollars per day. Of course, you could add your own cash, but the average minor leaguer doesn't have it like that. And if he doesn't, getting a square meal takes creativity.

In the majors, players are issued sixty dollars per day for meals on the road. If Galligani had a chance at that kind of money, his diet would change to match the new funds. So would pitcher Derek Manning's. "I could handle sixty dollars per day," Manning said gladly. "I'd eat the best food possible. I'd be lazy and order room service."

In defense of the major leaguers, all of their money doesn't go into their pouches. Some of it is used to pay the clubhouse workers who provide meals for them after the game. The players also tip the clubhouse staff for washing their clothes. And when it's time to chow, the major leaguers spend their time eating at the plush hotels they're staying in. In some of these places, buttered toast and dry cereal may cost fifteen dollars.

But this is the minor leagues, and creativity and careful planning are the keys in filling a player's stomach.

First, they want to get more bang for their bucks so they can stop the hunger pangs. Instead of blowing their cash at a fast food burger dive or loading up on junk food at the nearest service station, many of the players scanned the yellow pages for the all-you-can eat buffets.

Manning was one of the leaders of that pack. "I go to buffets so I can get a good meal and stay away from fast food as much as possible," he said. "I only eat two meals per day. I take every meal deal I can find. I always overspend, so I always bring an extra forty dollars to make sure I have enough money."

Then there are the chance takers. "I don't have a secret. I just eat twice a day whenever I can," Galligani said. "I usually have to go to the ATM. I don't worry about the cost. I try to eat as well as I can."

Eating right all of the time can be a problem sometimes. Some of that has to do with the cash allotted and the lack of transportation to get a decent meal when everything is closed after a game. Sometimes a quick run to the concession stand or a late night pizza is the best that is available.

This type of meal plan isn't always the best for top athletes. "In the offseason the team sends us pamphlets about sticking to good nutrition," Manning said, "but during the season we're given fifteen bucks, and sometimes it's tough to eat nutritious food."

Clubhouse Chatter

If it's a practical joke, chances are catcher Willie Morales is the one behind it. Ask outfielder Tony Banks, who felt Morales' wrath in midseason.

"Practical jokes help us get through the season," said the articulate Morales. "We try to make each other laugh by just being silly. It really means something when you know a guy. That makes the joke funnier."

Throughout the season, Morales joked with Banks about using so much Flex-All sports ointment that he started calling him Flex-All. The moniker also sparked a practical joke.

Banks received an empty box addressed to him at Old Kent Park. Attached was a letter that read: "I hope this letter and package reach you before you've absolutely fallen apart. I understand that you're the 'old man' on the ball club, and that you're starting to 'show signs.' I've sent this package because I want to keep you healthy. You see, I need healthy, strong men like you to represent (as an agent).

"I've taken many good athletes, including Mike Tyson, to the poor house, and I'd like to do the same for you. I want to be your agent. My services include the following: free Spice 1 and Snoop Doggy Dogg records and a ten-year contract with Flex-All 454.

"In return, I will expect only 50 percent of your salary. Please consider my offer. Sincerely, Don King."

"I know Tony pretty well," Morales said. "You have to be careful when you play jokes on people. You have to make sure that they'll take it well. Tony did."

◆ ◆ ◆

Willie Morales, voted the most popular Whitecap, powers one over the fence. Courtesy the *Grand Rapids Press*.

Morales' action on the field wasn't a joking matter. By the end of the season, the fans voted him the most popular Whitecap.

His talent was also admired by his father. Willie Morales Sr. remembered his son's early years vividly. "When I was playing college baseball, I looked over and saw Willie (Jr.) with my face mask on. He was barely two years old. I really got a kick out of that."

Morales Sr. has been getting a kick out of his son ever since that day when Junior wanted to be like Dad. Junior still wants to be like Dad. He credits most of his success to his father's guidance. "I learned everything from him first,"

Morales Jr. said. "He meant everything. I learned different things about the game from him at a young age."

Morales displayed some of that early tutelage in a game at Madison witnessed by his father on August 7. That's when he went four for five, scored twice, and had two doubles and a homer with three RBI's. In May at Old Kent Park, Morales Jr. slammed a homer in his father's presence.

"In college (University of Arizona) I was used to seeing him there every game," Morales Jr. said. "Now I only see him every now and then, so of course I'm going to get a little excited in playing when he's around."

Morales Sr. was a three-sport high school star in Tucson, Arizona. He was drafted by the New York Yankees out of high school, but instead enrolled at the University of Arizona. After a year, he transferred to Southern California College. After graduating, Morales Sr. played a year of baseball in the Mexican League. He coached amateur baseball for several years and now is a part-time scout for the Montreal Expos.

During Junior's youth, Senior said that he never pushed his son. "Playing baseball and catching is what Willie always wanted to do," Morales Sr. said. "I didn't push him. He pushed me. I would come home from work dead tired, and Willie would want me to throw him some pitches. There I was pitching to Willie, and his mother would be in the outfield."

Sleepwalking

This wasn't much of a practical joke, but first baseman Steve Cox and outfielder David Keel were able to smile about it.

It probably isn't wise to invite Keel to sleep overnight. Cox will attest to that. For the past two seasons, Cox has been awakened during the night by Keel, and each time Cox was in disbelief.

"Last year (at Southern Oregon) in the middle of the night, I was laying in bed," Cox said. "I rolled over because I felt something. He (Keel) was on his hands and knees, looking down at me. I was surprised, but I grabbed him and kicked him away. I asked him what the hell he was doing. He said, 'I don't know. I was only going to be there for a minute.'"

Keel did some more sleepwalking on the Whitecaps' road trip to South Bend in April, with the same results. Cox also said that Keel talks in his sleep. "He talks so much," Cox said. "One time he said, 'They want me down there.' I woke him up, but he insisted that he was awake."

Keel tried to explain. "I sleepwalk a lot. One time I woke up and threw a lamp across the room. Another time I woke up on my hands and knees, and I was ripping a sheet to threads. I don't know why I sleepwalk. I guess no one should ever be my roommate," he said with a smile.

When fully awake before games, Keel, a native of Huntsville, Alabama, was the butt of locker room jokes. He has an exercise routine that uses martial arts techniques to help him in baseball. "I hear it from the guys all of the time," Keel said. "All I'm doing is breathing exercises. Some things do look a little strange. They'll call me Bruce Lee."

Keel got involved with the martial arts during his first year in the Arizona League. "I've gotten faster and more flexible since I've learned it," said Keel about the art of Teng-

David Keel dusts off after a close play at second.
Courtesy the *Grand Rapids Press*.

soo Do, Aikido, and Muay Thai. "I'm not an expert. I've just picked up a few things."

◆ ◆ ◆

Trying to pick up the truth from pitchers Tim Kubinski and Ryan Whitaker could be difficult. Take for instance this debate during one road trip.

Two years ago in the playoffs of the Cape Cod League, a summer league for collegiate players, Whitaker's and Kubinski's teams were facing each other in the semifinals. The score was 1-1 in the thirteenth inning with Whitaker on the mound and Kubinski at the plate.

Kubinski was the pitcher and designated hitter for his

club. Coming to bat with the bases loaded and no outs, he was down in the count 0-2. Then he hit a single that scored the winning run. Kubinski also earned the win.

Now this is where the story differs from player to player. "He hit a jam shot off his thumbs, and our infield was in because we knew we had a slow runner at the plate," said Whitaker, with Kubinski yelling in the background to tell his side. "It never got out of the infield. A pretty good wind was blowing behind the ball. If the wind wasn't blowing, the ball would've landed by second base.

"That had to be the highlight of his baseball career. I thought for awhile it was going to get him a spot in the majors.

Tim Kubinski burns one over the plate.   Courtesy the *Grand Rapids Press.*

But since I broke his thumbs on the pitch, he decided not to hit anymore."

Kubinski, however, said Whitaker's story wasn't quite the way things actually happened. "When I got to the plate, the place was going nuts," Kubinski said while trying to keep a straight face. "Then the other team brought in this new kid (Whitaker). I never heard of him. I looked up his stats, and it said he was from Broken Arrow, Oklahoma, so I figured he wasn't that good.

"He tried to sneak a fastball by me. I hit it right back up the middle, and he hit the deck. I thought it was going to hit him in the head. Whitaker did an alright job, but he was overmatched."

♦ ♦ ♦

On another bus trip, manager Jim Colborn thought he was on the wrong bus. When he realized he was in the right place, he cracked a wide smile.

Whitecaps outfielder David Keel, second baseman Jason McDonald, catcher Randy Ortega, and catcher Willie Morales had all cut their hair very short. McDonald was completely shaven, Ortega and Keel had close shaves, and Morales' hair was the longest of the bunch, but still very close.

"I thought I was getting ready to lose them to the military," Colborn said. "I thought they all got their papers to be inducted into the service. Either that or they were on death row. I'd consider doing it myself, but I'd be afraid that it wouldn't ever grow out again."

Ortega was the barber responsible for the close shaves. Morales didn't get his as close as the others because he was trying for a certain look. "My hair is going to grow into what's called the Henry Rollins look," Morales said. "He was the former lead singer of Black Flag. Now he's the lead singer of the Rollins Band."

♦ ♦ ♦

The music selection of the Whitecaps was as varied as the four seasons. Sounds from the clubhouse ranged from rap to country. But before every Whitecaps game, the starting pitcher got to choose his note. Scott Baldwin's taste wasn't the most popular on the team.

"On my day I'll have country music," said Baldwin, holding cassettes of Mark Chesnutt, Toby Keith, and David Allan Coe. "The guys don't really like this much at all. But to keep them happy, I'll let Jason McDonald throw in some rap about fifteen minutes before we go onto the field. We call it the country-rap combo. They've started to like country a little, and I've started to like some rap."

When Tim Kubinski pitched, he popped in a tape of Pearl Jam or Metallica. Derek Manning's favorite was the Grateful Dead.

Killing More Time

During a rainout early in the season, Whitecaps manager Jim Colborn reflected on rain delays he had experienced in the major leagues. "We played a lot of cards, and some guys went out on the field and ran onto the tarp," Colborn said. "One time we were sliding in the outfield. My uniform was all muddy and wet, and I walked back into the clubhouse and this reporter came down. I hugged him and he got soaked and muddy. Later on he sent me the (laundry) bill."

During a rain delay against the New York Mets in 1970, Colborn was a wanted man. Pitching for the Chicago Cubs, he entered in relief during the fourth inning. The game was delayed in the seventh inning because of rain. When play was ready to resume, Colborn was missing in action.

Colborn explained. "In Shea Stadium, you walk from the bullpen into a tunnel (underneath the stands) that takes you into the clubhouse. So I was warming up to go back into the game, and then I walked back along the tunnel by myself."

While Colborn was strolling through the tunnel, the game was ready to resume. Everyone knew this except for the tunnel dweller. "Nobody in the park knew where I was," Colborn said. "For a second they thought they had the game started, but no pitcher. I was making my way to the dugout, and I knew the game was going to start, but not right then. (Cubs manager) Leo Durocher was screaming, 'Where's Colborn?' and they had guys running all over looking for me."

Colborn eventually made it back to the mound. He also earned the victory, which happened to be on his birthday.

There was also an incident while Colborn was a pitching coach for the Iowa Cubs, a Class AAA team in Des Moines. On this day, the rain and winds were so strong that the tarp on the field blew high across the backstop. Once the weather became too severe, fans in a restaurant at the park were told to take cover.

"All the players were in the clubhouse in the shower, and here come all of these fans from the restaurant," Colborn said. "They yelled for everyone to get out of the shower, and right then people started coming in."

◆ ◆ ◆

To help break them out of a funk during a dismal road trip, the Whitecaps played an intrasquad game with a sponge ball before facing Kane County. Players played out of position, and pitchers got to bat. Manager Jim Colborn pitched for one team, and pitching coach Gil Patterson (who threw a no-hitter) pitched for the other. Although neither team scored, pitcher Chris Michalak (who played center field) led both squads with two hits.

Michalak said he did everything he could for his team. "I'm swinging the bat well," said Michalak, who tried to look serious. "Colborn has a tough release point, but I was able to pick it up. Things went my way today, and hopefully it'll continue."

Marcel Galligani, who was player-manager for the losing squad, said his team played hard. "My team really battled, but with the pitchers at the beginning of the lineup, the non-athletes, that really hurt us," said Galligani in his best managerial impression. "But I must commend (pitcher) Jason Rajotte hitting the ball with a man on third base. That was a valiant effort. We only played three innings. We'll get them in the next six."

◆ ◆ ◆

When it came to fast eating and being well groomed, no one came close to pitcher Zack Sawyer. He was the bread and orange champion. Before games, several Whitecaps competed to see who could eat an orange and slice of bread the fastest. Sawyer downed an orange in seven seconds and a slice of bread in nineteen.

Sawyer also never got caught with things out of place. The right-handed pitcher was the only Whitecaps player who traveled with a hair dryer. "I've been that way all my life," said Sawyer, who has a Woody Woodpecker tattoo on his left shoulder and Stimpy, from the cartoon Ren and Stimpy, on his right shoulder. "I don't like hats. The only time I wear them is when I'm playing. I like to be presentable at all times. You never know who you're going to meet."

When pitcher Derek Manning first met Sawyer in spring training, he wasn't sure what to think of his new teammate. "One day we got out of the shower and he was fixing his hair," said a grinning Manning. "He had four different kinds of gels with him. I told Zack that he was polluting his hair and it would fall out.

"I don't see the purpose of drying your hair," Manning said. "If you're going to use all of that gel, it's going to make it look wet anyway."

Near Perfect

Jim Colborn didn't let being a manager kill the sense of humor that he developed as a player in the major leagues. The fun followed him to the minors as a manager.

A commercial for a local department store was shot at Old Kent Park in June. The spot, which involved Colborn and several players, aired on Father's Day.

Colborn said he was never involved with sales advertising during his ten years as a major-league hurler. He was never able to pitch a product that he supported. "I always wanted to do a Trojan condom commercial," said Colborn, trying to keep a straight face. "Doing this commercial was fun. I had to wear makeup for the first time, which was unusual, because I always thought I was perfect. I guess I'm not."

Colborn's imperfection showed as early as his high

Jim Colborn makes his point with umpire Stephen Willard.
Courtesy the *Grand Rapids Press*.

school days in California. The year was 1962, Ventura High School vs. Santa Paula High. With the score tied in the last inning, senior catcher Jim Hibbs stepped to the plate. "That was the only time I faced (Colborn)," Hibbs said. "I got the hit that beat him, and I never let him live it down. I got the winning hit to right, and he sucked up the loss."

Hibbs, who later was Colborn's teammate in the Pacific Coast League, visited the Whitecaps during the season at Fort Wayne. He played eight years in the minors before hanging it up and is now executive director of Ventura College.

Colborn, however, remembered that high school game differently. "(Hibbs) was ready to go to Stanford, and I was in the eighth grade," Colborn said. "They put me in to pitch against the league champions. I don't know if the ball (Hibbs hit) made it to the outfield grass."

Colborn faced many batters in his major league career, including several future and present Hall of Famers. But when asked which batter gave him the most trouble, Colborn didn't have to search too far for an answer. "John Lowenstein of the Baltimore Orioles. I kept him in the league for several more years. (Baltimore manager) Earl Weaver only used him against me, and he hit .800 off of me. He hit everything I threw to him."

The laughter, however, did stop momentarily for Colborn.

Brad Robinson had driven on U.S. 131 so many times that he probably could do it with his eyes closed. On one rainy day his eyes could've been shut for good. Robinson, a vender at Old Kent Park, was driving home after an April 30 Whitecaps game that was suspended because of rain. While reaching for his umbrella in the back seat, he lost control of his car. The 1988 Corsica slid and flipped on its hood into a ditch.

Colborn saw the accident from close range. "(Pitching coach) Gil (Patterson) and I were headed to the Charlevoix

Club to work out," Colborn said. "I noticed a car in front of us lose control and go off into the grass. All I could think of was blood and guts. I thought I'd have to pull him out because I was the first car."

As Colborn ran down to help, Robinson crawled out, and Colborn took him to his own car. Colborn then flagged down other cars for help. Robinson, a sophomore at Ottawa Hills High School, escaped unscathed.

"Before I got out of my car, I asked God for help," Colborn said. "I was praying that everything was all right. I don't feel like a hero, because lots of people stopped. I just got to him first."

Robinson was pleased with that. "I haven't had a chance to really thank him," he said. "I plan to do that soon."

The Fun Continues

During the first road trip to Springfield, the Whitecaps were introduced to the worst kind of heckler in sports — the know-it-all fan.

David Sheppard, who claimed that the inventor of the knuckleball had taught him everything about baseball, attended batting practice at Lanphier Park and freely shared his expertise with the Whitecaps. He offered unwanted advice on how the Whitecaps could improve their hitting and pitching. He even lent manager Jim Colborn some advice. The hottest tip was the one he gave first baseman Steve Cox.

Sheppard told Cox to put all of his weight on his back

foot before swinging. When Cox told him that the advised batting stance was uncomfortable, the fan said he'd better get used to it if he wanted to play in the majors. Cox doubled over in laughter. Somehow, Sheppard compared hitting to bowling, and pitching to fishing.

Ernie Harwell

The owner of the Atlanta Crackers minor league team thought he got the deal of the century.

In 1948, the Crackers picked up a catcher in a trade with the Brooklyn Dodgers. The only thing the Dodgers got in return was a seldom-used rookie, a radio announcer by the name of Ernie Harwell. That trade forty-six years ago put Harwell in the record books as the only radio announcer to be traded for a player.

Harwell, who later became the legendary voice of the Detroit Tigers, visited Old Kent Park for the Freedom Shrine dedication late in the year.

"I came home (to Atlanta) from the Marines, and I began to announce games for the Crackers," Harwell said. "The Dodger broadcaster (Red Barber) became ill on a trip. Brooklyn owner Branch Rickey contacted (Cracker owner) Earl Mann and wanted me to replace Barber. Mann agreed, but he wanted Cliff Dapper, a (minor league) catcher from Montreal, in exchange."

The rest is history. Dapper played for only a few years after the trade and eventually became the Crackers' manager.

Harwell, however, went on to a glorious broadcasting career. He was inducted into the Baseball Hall of Fame in 1986.

With the Whitecaps involved in a pennant race, any added boost could help the club — like a trade of Rick Berkey, who announced their games on WOOD-AM. "If we traded Rick, we'd have to include cash, a player to be named later, and bag of used baseballs," Colborn said.

Elvis Sightings

Late in the season, Bellingham (Oregon) manager Mike Goff made sports blooper highlights by dropping his pants and mooning an umpire during a game against Southern Oregon.

Whitecaps second baseman Eric Martins was with Southern Oregon that day before getting the move up to West Michigan in August.

Martins remembered Goff storming out of the dugout to dispute the umpire's call of a fair ball down the first base line. "He got in the ump's face and started bumping him," Martins said. "He was tossed out, and then right when he was about to walk away, he just dropped his pants. The crowd went crazy. I was on the bench laughing. I've seen managers get upset and go ballistic, but I've never seen anything like that in my life of playing baseball."

The Seattle Mariners (the parent club) suspended Goff indefinitely for his actions.

Elvis lives. At least he did at Old Kent Park and on the Whitecaps' road trips.

Elvis was a cardboard image of a hitter used by the Whitecaps pitching staff when warming up in the bullpen. Pitching coach Gil Patterson came up with the idea the previous season at Madison, and it has been a hit ever since.

"One day I was traveling and I saw a cardboard image of Michael Jordan," Patterson said. "I thought to myself that something like that would be good for our pitchers. I told Doc (trainer Brian Thorson), and he cut out an image."

Patterson said the point of the image is to help pitchers visualize a batter at the plate while working on different pitches. What made Elvis an even bigger star with the pitchers took place in 1993.

"Before a game last year, pitcher Stacy Hollins (now with Modesto) was throwing in the bullpen before the game," Patterson said. "Right before he finished, he threw a pitch that split Elvis in half. Hollins threw a no-hitter that day. Now, every pitcher tries to break Elvis in half. Whenever they do, they put him on Doc's training table."

◆ ◆ ◆

West Michigan's Matt Walsh had some fond memories of his two years of pitching for Boston College. One of them wasn't so wonderful, but it was an occasion that he'll never forget.

Waiting to start against Seton Hall, Walsh got the sign to make his way to the mound. "It was kind of cold that day and I had a light jacket on," Walsh said. "I sat down and got a drink of water. My jersey was on the hook behind me. Then I got the call to come in."

In the excitement, Walsh rushed out to the field without his jersey. He had on a long sleeve tee shirt. "I got halfway to the mound and my coach called me over," Walsh said. "He didn't say anything. He just looked down and started laughing. Then I noticed I didn't have my jersey on."

Once Walsh put on his jersey, he went on to defeat Seton Hall 3-2.

Around the Horn

After five hours, Quad City pitcher Billy Wagner began to worry. For the first time since giving her an engagement ring, he hadn't heard from his fiancée, Sarah Quesenberry, who was living in Pulaski, Virginia. They usually talked by telephone every night, especially before the day he pitched.

"When I finally got through," said Wagner with a somber look, "her mom told me what had happened. Sarah was in a car accident. I didn't sleep well last night. I was worried all day."

But Wagner, the Houston Astros' first choice in the 1993 draft, still managed to whiff eleven West Michigan Whitecaps and allow only one hit in his six complete innings. Quad City went on to a 5-1 victory before 6,240 fans at Old Kent Park in an afternoon game on May 12.

It was the Whitecaps' eighth loss out of their last eleven games, and second consecutive in a ten-game homestand. The Whitecaps remained at the bottom of the Northern Division at 15-17. Quad City was 15-16 in the Southern Division.

During his restless night, Wagner was reassured that his future bride was doing fine. She didn't suffer any major injuries in the accident, and she was resting at home.

Manager Jim Colborn hands the ball over to reliever Ryan Whitaker in a disastrous outing with Quad City. Courtesy the *Grand Rapids Press*.

Despite the stressful situation, Wagner had managed to perform. "I think it helped me a little bit to go on and throw," said Wagner, whose fastball was clocked at 95 mph. "My pitching coach (Gary Lucas) said it's hard being away in times like this, but it's better to go out and pitch because it can free your mind."

Wagner needed peace of mind early on, walking three consecutive Whitecaps in the first inning. With no outs, he struck out the next two batters and forced Randy Ortega to fly out to end the inning. The Whitecaps went down empty-handed.

In a jam that would make most pitchers' knees turn into jelly, Wagner remained focused because he was in familiar territory. "I've been in that situation so many times, because I'm a strikeout pitcher," said Wagner, who was drafted out of

Ferrum College in Virginia. "Either I strike the guy out, make him hit into an out, or walk in the run. I've done that so many times in college and in this league. I don't put any extra pressure on myself. I try to do what needs to be done, and it just happens."

What happens most of the time leaves batters swinging at air. Wagner doesn't try to hide what got him drafted. "If a hitter doesn't think fastball when facing me, he's crazy," he said. "I made it here with my fastball. If I'm going any higher, it'll be because of my fastball."

And how was that fastball? "You have to be able to react a lot quicker," said Whitecaps first baseman Steve Cox, who struck out three times. "You have to try to see it and hit it. I just saw it a little bit. It was a real tough day."

Added Mark Moore, "It's difficult to hit him, because you don't see that every day. He throws hard. When someone throws like that, you don't have enough time to react. You're not as relaxed."

For four straight innings, Wagner had the Whitecaps swinging in the breeze, or popping up for outs. He didn't give up a hit until Jose Guillen singled in the fifth.

After Wagner left after the sixth, the Whitecaps managed to squeeze out their only run in the seventh when Vinny Francisco singled in Ortega.

The loss, which included five Whitecaps errors, left an impression on Cox. "Nothing is going right," Cox said. "But things happen like that. We'll be out of the cellar as soon as we hit the ball."

That is something Wagner doesn't want to see when he's on the mound. "It was hard to come out here and pitch," said Wagner, who would go on to lead the league in strikeouts with 204. "But I was able to take out the frustration by pitching. Playing baseball is something I enjoy, and the good Lord has blessed me." And he also blessed that lightning fast arm.

◆   ◆   ◆

By the end of May and in the first two days of June, the Whitecaps found themselves in last place. During that time they visited Appleton, getting a chance to see firsthand what all the commotion was about in this town forty-five minutes south of Green Bay. Appleton is known as the hometown of the great escape artist Harry Houdini. Many years from now, it will also be known as the first professional stop of Alex Rodriguez, the number one overall pick in the 1993 amateur baseball draft.

The same scene follows Alex Rodriguez before and after every game. He doesn't need a script or tips from the director. He knows his role so well that he can see it vividly in his sleep.

Fans across the Midwest League remind Rodriguez every day that he was the Seattle Mariners' first draft pick, requesting autographs, poses for pictures, handshakes, or just his smile.

Rodriguez's teammate on the Appleton Foxes, pitcher Robin Cope, has seen the projected major league star sign a hoard of autographs routinely. "He's had an impact on this league that they haven't seen in a long time," Cope said. "Everywhere we go, people bring magazines, baseball cards, or anything with Alex's picture on it for him to sign.

"We went to Burlington, and I asked some fans how many games they'd been to this year. They said it was their first game. They didn't come to see the Bees, they came to see Rodriguez."

And when you see Rodriguez, you'll see a six-foot-three, two-hundred-pound shortstop with the grace of a ballerina in the field and the strength of a bull at the plate. In May Rodriguez was leading the Midwest League in homers with fourteen and was second in RBI's with forty-five. The best display of his power came when he hit ten homers and collected twenty-three RBI's in a ten-game stretch. In the field, however, he had sixteen errors in his first fifty-three games.

Quite aware of the high expectations, Appleton manager Carlos Lezcano wasn't worried about the negative numbers. "He's just eighteen years old," Lezcano said. "I don't care that some people think he should be perfect. He's coming along and playing better than what we expected. He'll be fine."

Things weren't always fine with Rodriguez in his quest for a major league baseball career. Baseball wasn't the original path he took as a freshman varsity basketball player at Christopher Columbus High School in Miami, Florida.

The spring of that year, Rodriguez decided to try out for the varsity baseball team. He was cut and relegated to the junior varsity. "Everyone said I was crazy to try out for baseball," remembered Rodriguez. "Everyone told me to stick with

Appleton's Alex Rodriguez is the Midwest League's top prospect.
Courtesy the *Grand Rapids Press*.

basketball, especially since I was getting letters from colleges as a ninth grader."

He was also told by Columbus baseball coach Brother Herb Baker that basketball was his best sport. "He told me that I didn't have it (for baseball), and that he already had a shortstop," Rodriguez said. "He said that I'd be on JV for the next three years, and by my senior year I might have a shot at varsity. That made me cry for days. From then on, I decided to put basketball on the back burner and decided it was baseball time."

The first step was when Rodriguez transferred to baseball power Westminster Christian High School, coached by Calvin College graduate Rich Hofman. Rodriguez made the varsity and finished his sophomore season with a .250 average

Rodriguez was pleased that Hofman had faith in him, but Hofman shocked him over the summer prior to his junior year. "With that batting average, I'm thinking that maybe people were right," Rodriguez said. "Then one day I'm reading the newspaper and there's an article where Hofman is quoted that by my senior year I'd be the number one pick in the baseball draft. It was the biggest confidence booster I've ever had. I never worked so hard in my life. I didn't want to let him down."

Hofman, who played three years of baseball for Calvin during the four-year span of 1962-66, has been around enough baseball to know talent. Since the Racine, Wisconsin, native became the coach at Westminster in 1969, he's won a state record 599 games. He's had twelve players drafted by the pros since 1983, and since 1980, sixty-five of his players have played college ball. Westminster won its fifth state championship in 1994 with a 34-4 record, and Hofman is only the ninth high school coach to be inducted into the American Baseball Coaches Hall of Fame.

So with that background, Hofman didn't believe he was

putting unwanted pressure on the young Rodriguez. "I'm a pretty straightforward guy. I've been doing this for a long time, and I think I can recognize talent," said Hofman, who played with current Calvin basketball coach Eddie Douma. "What I liked most about Alex was his work ethic. He was tall and lanky, and he was smooth on the field."

Hofman's praise was all the confidence Rodriguez needed. "I read those articles and felt it was time to go to work," Rodriguez said.

Work indeed. Rodriguez finished his three-year varsity career with a .419 batting average, seventeen homers, seventy RBI's, and ninety stolen bases. In thirty-three games of his senior year he batted .550, hit nine home runs, drove in thirty-six runs, and was thirty-five for thirty-five in stolen bases. He has been a member of the U.S. junior national team, and he became the first high school baseball player to receive an invitation to the U.S. National Team.

"Everytime I come back home, Brother Herb wants me to sign autographs for his baseball camps," Rodriguez said. "It's like 'Alex I love you. I'm so sorry you left.' He and I both know the true picture. He still gets a hard time from people in Miami (for letting Rodriguez transfer)."

Rodriguez's own hard times began after Seattle made him the first choice in the draft. Rodriguez was hoping to be drafted by the Los Angeles Dodgers, who were picking second, so he could play in front of his family when the Dodgers came to Miami during the season. He asked Seattle not to draft him, but they did, so he asked for $2.5 million. No draft choice had ever received higher than $1.55 million, so the salary demand led to a long, exhausting process.

Rodriguez, who also had intentions of attending the University of Miami, finally settled on a $1.3 million bonus, but a hearing was still pending, filed over the summer by the Major League Players Association and Rodriguez's agent Scott

Boras. The complaint accused the Mariners of coercing the high school graduate to sign a contract without fully explaining it to him.

There are any number of ways an arbiter could rule: Rodriguez could be declared a free agent and tossed back into the amateur draft; the Mariners could be ordered to pay Rodriguez more money; the contract could be declared valid and the whole thing forgotten.

Rodriguez just wants to play ball. "I'm signed, I'm here, and I'm lucky," Rodriguez said. "Things (the contract situation) could've been worse, and they could've been better. Now there's just one more step with the grievance. The negotiations took the glamour and excitement out of getting drafted, but I know it's a business. I'd rather learn it now than have my heart broken years from now."

While the contract was pending, Rodriguez pelted home runs and fielded ground balls. His rise as the next superstar was fast, almost overnight. The contract ordeal transferred him from a boy to a man, with the pressures that come with being the top choice. Rodriguez was happy to see the 1994 draft come along.

"I'm glad this year's draft is here," he said, with his patented smile. "Hopefully, some people will forget about me and let me do my thing until I get to the big leagues. This year's top pick will have the pressure now. Sometimes you want to have that feeling where you're sneaking up on people, but I haven't had that for three years." Thanks to Brother Herb.

Rodriguez didn't get to play in the Midwest League All-Star game at Fort Wayne. Just three days before the game, Rodriguez, who was in the top three in several Midwest League offensive categories, was promoted to Class AA Jacksonville. His last game in the Midwest League was a nothing for four performance against West Michigan at Old Kent Park on June 14.

In his first at bat for the Jacksonville Suns, playing in Greenville, South Carolina, Rodriguez hit a home run against the Greenville Stars.

"I'm excited," said Rodriguez by telephone from Greenville. "I'm still in a state of shock. Carlos (Appleton manager Lezcano) called me into his office before our game and told me to pack my bags because I was moving up." A spot was made for Rodriguez when Jacksonville shortstop Andy Sheets was moved to Class AAA in Calgary, Alberta.

Rodriguez was joining another popular rookie in the Southern League. "I'm pretty hyped to meet Michael Jordan," said Rodriguez about the former NBA star. "I'll try to get his autograph for my brother."

The move to Class AA was eventful for Rodriguez, but nothing could top his three-week stint in the major leagues. He made his debut with Seattle against the Boston Red Sox at Fenway Park in July.

After just four months in the minors, Rodriguez's jump to the big leagues brought mixed reactions at Old Kent Park.

Whitecaps Juan Dilone was elated when he heard the news. "That was great news — just one more Dominican in the big leagues," said Dilone about Rodriguez, whose parents were born in the Dominican. "I'm happy for him because he's a friend. With him making it, that gives me motivation that one day I may be there."

Infielder Vinny Francisco, also of the Dominican Republic, said he wasn't surprised that the eighteen-year-old Rodriguez made the jump so soon. "I'm not surprised, because he can hit in any league," Francisco said. "When I first saw him, I knew it wouldn't take long for him to be in the big leagues."

Whitecaps manager Jim Colborn was surprised about the promotion, but he also understood. "The pressure of winning in the big leagues overcame Seattle's desire to develop the guy until he was ready," Colborn said. "It's another case of rushing a player to the big leagues, which is a sign of desperation."

Colborn never questioned Rodriguez's talent. He saw a player with good baseball instinct, and someone who would make the necessary adjustments at the top level. "His defense will hurt the team a little bit," Colborn said. "He could make twenty errors before the season is over by playing every day. That's the exact same thing the Cubs did to Shawon Dunston. He went from Class A ball to the majors, and he wasn't ready. You could see his talent, but he wasn't ready for that level yet."

Cedar Rapids manager Tom Lawless saw something special in Rodriguez during his brief time in Class A. "He was way above everyone in this league," Lawless said. "He won't embarrass himself in the majors, but he also won't do up there what he did down here. Defensively, he's as good as anyone they have up there. Offensively, he'll probably struggle a little bit. But you never know until he gets there."

Jack Spencer, a high school baseball coach in Jacksonville, Florida, and the baseball chairman of that state, saw the move of Rodriguez to the majors as a step in the right direction for Seattle. "He's truly a phenom," said Spencer, who was visiting Old Kent Park during a visit to his hometown, Muskegon. "It'll be amazing if we see a player like him and Ken Griffey Jr. again in our lifetime. The tools that they have are incredible. Their size, strength, and their power are something else. I first saw Rodriguez as a tenth grader. I knew right then he was going to be something special."

◆ ◆ ◆

A couple of Rodriguez's Appleton teammates were special in their own right.

At the age of thirty, Delwyn Young was the oldest player in the Midwest League. He was actually slated as a player-coach, but it should have be more like coach-player. "I didn't come here to play. I came here to coach," Young said. "But when our third baseman got injured, it put us down a player. Since I came here as a player-coach, and since no one was ready to be sent here, they activated me."

This old dog may not know any new tricks, but he could certainly still hit. The Whitecaps found that out during one game, as Young, who was hitting .306 in fourteen games, went three-for-four with a double.

"He knows so much about the game," said Foxes pitcher Robin Cope. "One game before he went up to bat, he said he was going to hit a home run, and he did. Another time he said he was going to hit one out, and he got a double off the wall. We got on him for that."

Young has played in the minors for twelve years. He was the Cincinnati Reds' second pick in the 1981 draft. His up-and-down career, which now has him in the Seattle Mariners organization, has sent him to Cleveland, Montreal, Philadelphia, Detroit, and Taiwan.

After hundreds of broken promises of call-ups to the majors and several injuries, Young finally settled on becoming a player-coach. After sitting out a year, and ready to give up the game he loves, Young's father, a scout for the Mariners, asked his son to assist him with a tryout camp. That's where Young bumped into an old colleague.

"I went to the camp and signed a contract to be an associate scout," said Young, who looked several years younger than his actual age. "Then I'm introduced to the head scout of organization. He looks at me and says, 'Hey, wait a minute. I know you. You can play.'"

So he went to spring training and started bopping the ball all over the place. He also injured his elbow, preventing him from throwing consistently. The Mariners then offered him a position as a player-coach on the Class A level. They also promised that he might be moved to AA or AAA if things worked out.

Things did work out in Class A. But Young's biggest asset for the Foxes was on the player level. "I relate to them," Young said. "They give me respect as a coach, but they also respect me as a player because I can get in there and show them."

Married with five children, Young believed he still had the ability to play in the major leagues. Still, he wasn't getting any younger. He could still make it, but more than likely it would be as a coach.

"It doesn't matter to me. Either coach or player is fine," Young said. "I've played with some great players, and I've played some great years of baseball. God has a plan for everybody. I can't dwell on what could've happened. I do know that I've given this game a lot of my time. I've given it my all. I was just in the wrong places at the wrong time."

♦ ♦ ♦

Time indeed. The opportune time for Appleton catcher Jose Cueller finally came in 1994.

But in order for that moment to come, he had to defect from Cuba to the United States in the summer of 1993. Making it to this country for Cueller was something right out of a spy magazine.

Cueller was a member of the Cuban Class C National Team (A is the highest level), playing a tournament on an island off the Cuban coast. After the tourney ended his team left, but Cueller hid and stayed behind, with the assistance of some people in the stands. He then made contact with his family, who had escaped Cuba in 1980 and were living in

Florida, and they (mother, father, sisters, and brothers) hired a boat that picked him up and brought him to Florida.

Later, Cueller contacted an agent who helped him sign with the Seattle Mariners.

More Money

A *Wisconsin State Journal* story about twenty-one-year-old Scott Kelly made him so popular that he was getting hand cramps from signing autographs. Despite the pain, Kelly enjoyed every minute.

Well, the story wasn't exactly about Kelly. It was about his alter ego. Kelly was better known as Madcap, the Madison Hatters' mascot.

Kelly, or Madcap (a mouse dressed in a tuxedo and top hat), was reported as making more money per home game than the average Class A baseball player — the only mascot who made more than the players. For each game Kelly worked, he was paid $50. The players, on the other hand, earned about $950 a month. The Hatters averaged $32.82 per home game.

That fact brought plenty of stink from some Madison players. "I haven't heard anything directly from the players," said Kelly, a political science graduate at the University of Wisconsin. "Indirectly, I've been told to stay away from the dugout. Someone left a message at the office with only two words — 'hot foot.' It hasn't been too bad, but I have avoided them (the players)."

Reaction from the Madison players was mixed, from

those who supported Madcap to those who felt Kelly's act wasn't worth a dime. Those against his salary made nasty comments, but some, like Jason McDonald, said more power to him. "It's not that big of an issue," McDonald said. "Players on this level know coming in that we don't make a lot of money. That gives us more incentive to move up to make more."

Kelly also couldn't figure out the big deal. Besides, working as a mascot didn't pay the rent. It was basically spare change. He worked full-time as a video clerk while searching for a job in politics. "It would be nice to do this full time for a major league team," said Kelly, who signed on as mascot in the final two weeks of last season. "That would probably be the perfect job for me because I've been told that I'm strange. I have Muppets all over my room, and I have a poster of the Philly Fanatic on my wall. I have a long way to go for that. I'm not counting on it, but that would be nice."

Of the fourteen teams in the Midwest League, thirteen had mascots. In West Michigan, Burlington, Peoria, and Springfield, the mascot earned twenty-five dollars per game. Fort Wayne paid twenty-three dollars a game, followed by Beloit and South Bend (twenty), Quad City (seventeen), Rockford (sixteen), and Appleton (five). Clinton's mascot was paid minimum wage, while Kane County wouldn't release its figures. Cedar Rapids was the only league team without a mascot.

Midwest Trotter

When it came to travel in the Midwest League, no one knew the roads better than Springfield bus driver Rosy Hester, forty-nine, of Davenport, Iowa.

Hester has driven Midwest League teams since 1969. That was the year he was the main driver for three different teams at the same time, driving for Quincy, Danville, and Decatur, teams no longer in the league. "When I'd dropped one off, I'd pick the other team up," remembered Hester, who resembles a jazz musician more than a long-time bus driver. "They weren't home at the same time, so it wasn't that big of a deal."

Hester has fond memories of a time when he drove players like former major league stars Bruce Sutter, Pat Burke, and Bill North. Hester became so intoxicated with the league that he set up a hall of fame of sorts in his basement, filled with memorabilia from past and present, including uniforms and pictures.

Hester expressed pride in busing this league. "Grand Rapids should also be proud to be in this league," he said. "The Midwest League has produced more major league players than any other minor league. Over 350 current players in the majors played in this league. I've enjoyed being a part of this."

◆ ◆ ◆

Eddie Hartwell also enjoyed being in the Midwest League. He couldn't say the same about his student days at Notre Dame. Despite SAT scores well over 1,100 and offers turned down from schools like Amherst, Columbia, and Princeton, Hartwell was still stigmatized.

"Being black with a little size at Notre Dame led people

to believe that I was a football player," said Hartwell, a six-foot, two-hundred-pound outfielder for the Clinton LumberKings. "It got nerve-racking. Why did I have to be labeled and stereotyped as a football player all of the time because of my race and size?"

The stigma wasn't limited to campus. The assumption followed him to social gatherings. "I'd go to parties, and people would only want to talk to me about sports," Hartwell said. "I'd tell them that they could go to something else, because I could carry a conversation about other subjects. People were surprised when they learned that I was at Notre Dame on an academic scholarship. Some didn't realize that I could think and comprehend."

Hartwell's experience wasn't much different than what many black students on predominately white campuses experienced. It was too often assumed that black students went to college merely to play sports with dreams of playing professionally. That wasn't the case for Hartwell, although he eventually did decide to play baseball.

Playing sports for Hartwell wasn't out of necessity. He played as a hobby. "I didn't plan on playing baseball after high school," Hartwell said. "But when I got to Notre Dame I met a guy who was trying out for the baseball team. He and I talked about it, and I decided to walk on. We both made it."

Hartwell set a Notre Dame single season record when he hit .447 as a senior in 1993. He also hit thirteen of his eighteen career homers that year and drove in sixty-eight runs. The native of Fort Worth, Texas, led the Irish into the NCAA regional along with West Michigan pitcher Chris Michalak. The Irish finished 46-16 that season and were runners-up in the regional.

Following graduation, Hartwell hit .382 in Rookie ball in the Giants organization, and then hit .226 at Everett last season. This year he hit .279 for the LumberKings.

Waiting their turn in the Whitecaps bullpen are (from left) Gustavo Gil, Marcel Galligani, Tim Bojan, Zack Sawyer, Mark Moore, and Matt Walsh. Courtesy the *Grand Rapids Press*.

Hartwell platooned in the outfield for Clinton, but the promotion of All-Star outfielder Benji Simonton to San Jose (higher Class A) gave him more playing time.

But even if he wasn't in the game plans, Hartwell remained at peace. He said nothing was as assuring for him as having a degree in his back pocket. "I see other guys' faces when they're having bad days and struggling. I'll hear them wondering about being released. I don't have a 'so what' attitude, but I can do something else (besides baseball). Some guys only have one direction, and I feel bad for them."

"It's nice to have something to fall back on," said Hartwell, who graduated from Notre Dame with a degree in marketing. He advised younger athletes to hit the books as hard as they play. "You're not invincible," Hartwell told youngsters. "Any given day something could happen, and your athletic career is gone and you need something to fall back on. Take education as seriously as you can. Be a competitor on and off the field."

No Pitchers Allowed

No matter how many strikeouts or wins they earn, something is always missing in the lives of Midwest League pitchers. They never get a chance to hit. Ever since the designated hitter was adopted by the American League in 1973, colleges and many minor leagues have followed suit in substituting another player to hit for the pitcher.

Whitecaps manager Jim Colborn pitched ten years in the majors, including stints in the American League. "I didn't miss hitting at first (after the rule was enacted)," said Colborn, "but after a while I did. I was such a good hitter. I hit .300 — I had three hits in ten years."

Pitcher Chris Michalak, a better example of a good hitter, was known to carry a big stick at Notre Dame. He hit .380 in his four-year career. His success at the plate included a three-for-four game during his sophomore year, also tying a Notre Dame record with six RBI's.

Michalak missed not being able to get a chance to hit. "Everyone wants to hit," he said. "Growing up, you dream about striking someone out and then hitting the winning home run."

Not being able to enter the batter's box also left pitcher Zack Sawyer dreaming. "The last time I hit was in high

99

school," said Sawyer, who hit four homers in one high school contest. "I felt more into the game when I knew I was going to hit as well as pitch. There's no better feeling than hitting a home run. I really miss that."

Down Under and Over

It wasn't quite the reminder of home that catcher Lyall Barwick was looking for during the first inning of a game between Cedar Rapids and West Michigan in April.

On a play at home, Whitecaps second baseman Jason McDonald barreled into Barwick, who was protecting the plate. Barwick lay on the dirt for ten minutes before being escorted to the dugout. "I played (Australian Rules) football," Barwick said, "but that was the hardest hit I've ever felt. I thought my shoulder was broken."

Barwick is one of many natives of Australia who play professional baseball in the United States. Although cricket and football are the top sports down under, baseball is rising in popularity, partly because of the Major League-backed Australian League formed four years ago.

The Kane County Cougars had two Australian-born players on their team. Australian players in the majors included Craig Shipley with the San Diego Padres and Graeme Lloyd and Dave Nilsson of the Milwaukee Brewers.

Barwick first saw baseball on television in the early 1980s. His interest led him to play in grammar school and on club teams while a teenager. He became a member of an

Australian team that traveled to Canada and the U.S. A tour through New Orleans changed his life.

"I was scouted by a junior college in Louisiana," Barwick said. "I played there for two years. I was drafted my first year and signed with the Angels as a free agent in 1992. So far, things have worked out for me."

First Half Slide

The Whitecaps finished sixth in the Northern Division (34-35) for the first half of the season. In the Midwest League, the 140-game season is cut in half (70 games each). A team has two chances to win its division to make the playoffs. However, if the first half winner also wins the second half, then the team that finishes in second place gets a playoff bid.

The final weeks before the mid-season All-Star break in June watched the Whitecaps slide, injuries pile up, and the baseball amateur draft begin. Some players also moved up to higher Class A Modesto, and manager Jim Colborn took four days off.

The Oakland Athletics ordered their minor league managers and coaches to take a four-day break during the season. Under the direction of pitching coach Gil Patterson and Brad Fischer, the assistant for player development for the parent team, the Whitecaps won three out of four games.

When Colborn returned to Old Kent Park, he had second thoughts. "When I heard that they were winning, I thought about staying home, because I didn't want to upset the apple cart," said Colborn, who attended his daughter Daisy's college graduation during his time off.

Moving Up

The Oakland organization spoiled West Michigan pitcher Steve Lemke's plans and scrambled his life for the next few days. Lemke, who had pitched his last nineteen innings without giving up a run and won his last three games, became the third Whitecaps player promoted. Word came on May 24 while the team was playing at Rockford.

The right-hander from Lincolnshire, Illinois, reported to Class AA Huntsville the following morning. Because injuries had cut into the Huntsville pitching staff, Lemke pitched one game in relief there before heading for Class A Modesto (a higher level than West Michigan), joining former Whitecaps pitcher Bob Bennett and infielder Jose Guillen.

Despite the hassle of traveling and rearranging plans, Lemke still craved this chance. "I had to make a lot of telephone calls home," said Lemke, who lived an hour and forty-five minutes from Rockford. "I had to tell my family not to come (to the game). I was scheduled to pitch today. They were coming to Kane County on the next road trip, and now I have to tell them not to come to that too.

"I have a lot of things going through my head," said Lemke, who finished at 4-2 with a 2.27 ERA for the Whitecaps. "I'm thinking about pitching against AA hitters, and then pitching in California."

Lemke also had to worry about his clothes and automobile in Grand Rapids. But before he got a chance to worry about anything else, he had to catch a flight and pitch only hours after landing in North Carolina, where the Stars were playing the Carolina Mud Cats. A day later Lemke flew across country to join the Modesto A's.

No matter how many frequent flier miles he piled up in the next forty-eight hours, Lemke wouldn't trade his opportunity away. He had a hunch that this day might be coming soon. "I had an idea that maybe I was going to get moved up," Lemke said. "Once you've played a few years, you start to get a feeling about things. Whenever Keith Lieppman (director of player development) is in town, things usually start to happen."

Right-hander Steve Lemke earned a spot with Class AA Huntsville.
Courtesy the *Grand Rapids Press.*

Before Lieppman arrived in Grand Rapids a week prior to the Whitecaps' trip to Rockford, Lemke was already showing the type of stuff pitching coaches like to see. "Of all the pitchers, he's the one that's throwing the best and is the most consistent," said pitching coach Gil Patterson. "He's able to execute the pitches that are needed to pitch at higher levels. All of our guys do it on occasion, but he's the one who's executing those things (consistently)."

Lemke agreed. "Every time I've been out, I feel I've done a good job," Lemke said. "Usually when that happens, the organization rewards you."

Mat Reese was disappointed that another close friend was leaving. "I'm happy for him, and I'm sad to see him go because he's a good friend of mine," Reese said. "But he has to get on with his life and his career. Hopefully, I can join him before the summer's over."

Along with Lemke's departure came a new Whitecaps pitching alignment. The eight-starter buddy system that paired the starters died, along with the seventy-pitch limit. In their place were a new rotation and a ninety-pitch limit. The new starting rotation included, in order, Derek Manning, Scott Baldwin, Chris Michalak, Tim Kubinski, and Matt Walsh. Former starters Tim Bojan and Zack Sawyer would join Ryan Whitaker, Jay Rajotte, and Steve Zongor in relief.

◆ ◆ ◆

Just before the All-Star break, another Whitecap got the nod. Pitcher Steve Zongor became the fourth Whitecap, and the third pitcher, promoted to Modesto.

Zongor left Michigan leading the team with nine saves, finishing at 2-1 with a 2.38 ERA. Opponents batted just .145 against him.

Zongor was surprised about his promotion. "During spring training, my thinking was that I'd move up near the end of the year," Zongor said. "As of late I've been pitching well, so I thought there was a chance. But I still thought things wouldn't happen until the end of the year." He would leave Grand Rapids and join his new team in San Jose, California, later that day.

The University of Kentucky graduate signed with the Athletics as an undrafted free agent. "I'm happy about the opportunity because it'll be a new challenge," Zongor said about the promotion. "It was bittersweet, because this has been a great place to play. I'm also leaving a lot of good friends behind."

One of those good friends was roommate Mat Reese. "I'm happy for him," said Reese, who had also roomed with Steve Lemke. "We spent a lot of free time together. I'm going to miss him. I hope I can join him there."

The Running Game

During his ten-year major league pitching career, there was one thing that West Michigan Whitecaps manager Jim Colborn despised. "Teams that ran drove me nuts," Colborn said. "I hated it. It was cheating when teams bunted and ran. I wished they'd just play baseball."

What once drove Colborn crazy now began to drive other teams up the wall. At the mid-season mark the Whitecaps were second in all of minor league baseball with 115 stolen bases. Augusta, a Class A team in the South Atlantic League, led with 121 steals.

Coincidentally, Pittsburgh Pirates base-running coach Jay Loviglio was behind Augusta's running game. He was the same man who taught Colborn about base stealing when the two worked in the Chicago Cubs' minor league system.

Colborn learned the importance of running, and learned it well. "It's the one element of the game that can infuse enthusiasm and aggressiveness," he said. "You can tell guys to be aggressive at the plate and in the field, but you can actually be aggressive running. It's the most fun for the players. They love to run."

Whitecaps infielder Jason McDonald certainly loved to run. His love kept him in the thick of the base-stealing race in the Midwest League. In the first seventy games, McDonald stole thirty-three bases. He credited Colborn's style to those numbers. "I like his style. It helps me. It's a big part of my game. It's helping me become a better player," McDonald said. "Jim lets us steal a lot. He's not afraid of letting the other team know that we're going to run and keep running until they stop us."

Lone Star

Sometimes Scott Baldwin appeared out of place, or at least from another time — especially when he strolled into view with his cowboy boots, hat, and his theme songs that blared in the West Michigan Whitecaps' clubhouse.

"My teammates give me crap about my country music and cowboy hats," Baldwin said. "Everyone on the team is a little different. It's good that everyone sticks to what they are. They laugh and say things, but they're going to listen to my country music, no matter what."

The Midwest League noticed more than Baldwin's western-style dress. The league managers voted him to represent the Northern Division in the thirtieth All-Star game.

Before 5,020 fans at Fort Wayne Memorial Stadium, the Southern Division defeated the North 3-2. Bob Henley (Burlington) was named the MVP for his game-winning hit in the sixth inning.

Baldwin (who was 4-4 at the break), was fifth in the league with seventy-seven strikeouts. He didn't play in the All-Star game. He also didn't complain. "I would've loved to pitch," Baldwin said. "You always want to face the best. But it's more important how the season goes and how my arm goes. It feels really good right now, so there was no since of pushing something. Being here is an honor, but I'm getting ready for the second half."

In the first half of the season, Baldwin was involved in two shutouts. He led the team with a season-high eight strikeouts in one game. Baldwin, a lefty who resides in Lewiston, Idaho, was drafted by Oakland in the thirteenth round of the 1993 draft. At Southern Oregon last year he was 3-3 with a 6.11 ERA and had forty strikeouts in fifteen games.

Before Southern Oregon, Baldwin attended Lewis-Clark State College. He married just before graduating. "We dated in high school," said Baldwin about his wife Staci. "Being away from her was a lot harder last year. This year we have a house, so she's back home (in Lewiston) taking care of that. She visits twice a month, and we talk on the telephone every few days."

Probably the only time Baldwin and Staci will spend the

kind of time together he craves is when he retires from baseball. By then, he hopes to have fulfilled a childhood fantasy. "When I grew up, we had five horses," Baldwin said. "I'd like to own a ranch one day in Idaho. But you have to have a lot of money to do that. Owning a big ranch and going big-game hunting for the rest of my life would make me happy."

Overcoming the Pain

First baseman Steve Cox was injured in May and sat out until July 3. In each of his three years as a professional baseball player, Cox has suffered a freak injury on the field causing him to miss valuable playing time.

The six-foot-four, two-hundred-pound Cox was hit in the eye by a ball during batting practice. It occurred while he was playing catch in the outfield. Cox's right cheekbone was fractured and three bones broken in the accident. This led to surgery, where a thin Teflon plate was placed below his eye to support it.

The Strathmore, California, native, who was drafted in the fifth round of the 1992 draft, recalled the incident that sidelined him. "Someone yelled 'heads up,' and I turned to see where the ball was. I saw it coming right at my face. It got me and I felt the swelling. I blew my nose, and blood came running out.

"The ball crushed the lower floor of my eye socket, and all of the blood ran into my sinuses. It's just another obstacle I'll have to go through. I was hurt, but I was so mad. It was

Injuries only increased first baseman Steve Cox's determination to show his stuff. Courtesy the *Grand Rapids Press*.

the third time in three years, and it just angered me that it happened again."

While lying on the ground, Cox's mind quickly reviewed the first two times he was hurt. The first time was during his first year of pro ball in the instructional league in Scottsdale. During a bunting drill, only two weeks into the season, Cox bunted at an inside pitch and the ball came off the end of his bat, hitting him in the nose.

"It was the first bloody nose of my life. It was also the first time I'd ever been hurt. I was seventeen years old and away from home. I had to have surgery to fix my broken nose," Cox said. "It was kind of embarrassing, because I had to get my parents' permission for the surgery because I was under eighteen."

Cox went from being embarrassed to angry the following year at Southern Oregon. Things started off well enough (he was hitting better than .300), but again he suffered a freak injury.

In the bottom of the ninth inning, with no outs and a runner on second, Cox found himself in a bunt situation. "The manager said he'd give me one strike to drive in a run or I'd have to bunt. With a 3-1 count, he gave me the go-ahead sign. It was a pitch up, and I swung hard. I heard something pop in my hand."

Cox strained ligaments in his hand and had to wear a cast for six weeks. "At this time I was frustrated," Cox said. "I'd had a great extended spring and I was swinging the bat great, and all of a sudden — bam! The doctors couldn't find out exactly what was wrong with me, but every time I picked up a bat it hurt."

Healed again, Cox came into this season with something to prove. His proving ground was spring training, when he hit five home runs in seven days.

When he got to Grand Rapids, he started slowly. But just

before his injury, as usual, he got hot. "The morning of my latest injury, I was thinking about all of the injuries and how they always happen when things are going good," Cox said. "When I was on the ground bleeding, I thought about that."

After this latest setback, however, Cox didn't feel sorry for himself. "I wasn't mad at myself, because there wasn't anything I could do about it," he said. "I wasn't feeling sorry for myself like Nancy Kerrigan by saying, 'Why me, Why me.' Why would this have to happen to anybody?"

But since it did happen again to Cox, he planned to use it as source of inspiration. "Now, I really have something to prove to myself," said Cox. "I play better under adversity. I'll come back strong from this. I just hope it doesn't happen again."

While waiting to heal, Cox did color commentary on Whitecaps' radio broadcasts with Rick Berkey.

Baseball Draft

The annual amateur baseball draft took place in June. Many dreams for young men across the country were either fulfilled or deferred.

Once a boy puts on a baseball uniform as a Little Leaguer, he imagines what it would be like to play professional baseball. West Michigan Whitecaps outfielder Tony Banks often wondered while growing up in Oakland, California, if he'd get his chance. It almost didn't happen.

In 1989 Banks graduated from Skyline High School with a .600 batting average, but without a scholarship offer. That year he was also invited to try out for a state All-Star team, but he was cut. Then he was spotted by a local junior college coach, who offered him a spot on his team.

After Banks' two years at Laney Junior College in Oakland, Nebraska was the only Division I program that offered him a scholarship. He wasn't that interested. He was shocked that he didn't get any other bids, so he waited.

Then a friend offered help. Cal State-Fullerton played Fresno State, and a Laney graduate there was giving Cal State fits. The Fullerton coach wanted to know if Laney had any more players of this type.

Enter Banks. "Cal State called me and offered a scholarship only if they lost a player to the draft, or if another recruited player decided not to come," Banks said. "I wanted to go there. They were closer to Oakland, and they had the same nickname of my high school (the Titans)."

Nebraska was still interested, and Banks tried to hold them off as long as he could. The Cornhuskers made a final offer, but Banks was still waiting for Cal State-Fullerton. "Then Cal State started to hear some things about me, and they decided to sign me," Banks said. "They never saw me play. They just took it on the word of a friend."

During his junior year, Banks noticed scouts at Cal State-Fullerton games. They weren't watching just him, but were scanning the entire roster. Then came the draft. Banks never heard his name called.

Banks didn't get a ring, possibly because tendinitis in his knee had limited him to designated hitter all season. "That had something to do with it," Banks said. "The scouts probably figured that I couldn't play any defense. So that summer I decided not to play any summer ball and to just heal. I was getting ready for the next draft." So Banks suffered yet one more setback, but just like before, he faced the challenge.

In June of his senior year, he again waited by the telephone. While trying to dodge calls from sleazy agents, and friends and family calling to ask if some team had called him, Banks began to get frustrated. "My mother came into the room quietly, because she knew what I went through last year," Banks said. "She noticed me looking at the television crazy. A program was discussing the day's picks."

Then Dorothy Banks made a suggestion, or more like a command. "She said for us to get down on our knees and pray," Banks said. "After five minutes of praying, the telephone rang. It was the Oakland A's telling me they had chosen me in the twenty-first round. My mother's prayers worked." And so did a little perseverance.

More Games

The second half of the Midwest League season began for West Michigan with an eight-game road trip against the Burlington Bees. The Whitecaps hoped to improve from a sixth-place, first-half finish in the Northern Division. But that wouldn't happen without more personnel changes and a return to the eight-man rotation buddy system.

Pitcher Chris Michalak was moved to Modesto (higher Class A). Michalak, who led the team with ten pickoffs, finished at 5-3 and a 3.43 ERA. "This is a happy and sad time," said Michalak, Notre Dame's all-time game-winning pitcher. "I'm happy because your goal is to move up. I'm sad because I'm going to miss some good friends and the good fans at Old Kent Park."

Three pitchers replaced Michalak and Steve Zongor, also promoted at mid-season. Bill King, Jason Beverlin, and Al Gogolin all joined the Whitecaps in Burlington, ready to get on with their professional baseball careers.

King, the Oakland Athletics' third pick in the 1994 draft, is a six-foot-five, 215-pound right-hander. At Birmingham Southern University he had sixty-seven strikeouts in eighty-seven innings with a 2.48 ERA. Beverlin, the A's fourth pick, is six-foot-five, 230 pounds, a righty from Western Carolina University. Gogolin is a six-foot-four, 215-pound right-hander from Georgia Tech. He was Oakland's thirteenth pick.

Gogolin, whose grandfather Al Gogolin Sr. resides in Grand Rapids, was excited about playing for the Whitecaps.

Chris Michalak fires away.   Courtesy the *Grand Rapids Press.*

"My grandfather is pumped up," Gogolin said. "He told me that I'll have my own cheering section. It's going to be a long road, but I'm ready to go."

Gogolin came with some championship experience. He was the starting pitcher in Georgia Tech's loss to Oklahoma in the finals of this year's College World Series.

Although he was still waiting for his first appearance in a Whitecaps uniform, he had already sought advice on the play at this level. "I talked to guys who've played on this level, and they said it was a step above college. If you're good in college, you should be able to do good here."

King hoped he'd be a do-gooder when he got his chance to take the mound for the Whitecaps. His first taste of the pros came at Medford (lower Class A), but it didn't last long.

"I was going to buy a car and have it shipped, but the scouting director (Dick Bogard) said I shouldn't do that because I'd probably only be in Medford for three games," King said. "From then on, I set that as my goal to get moved up. Luckily, it happened after one outing. I pitched three innings and gave up a walk and a single."

Rain postponed Beverlin's first chance to pitch for West Michigan. Even though the game at Burlington was rained out, he knew his dream of pitching professionally would finally come true. "I've wanted to be in this position since I was a kid," he said. "That's every player's dream. They wouldn't be playing unless it was. Playing here is a good first step."

Beverlin's steps have been good ever since he graduated from Dondero High School in Royal Oak, Michigan. From there he went to Western Carolina, where he led his team to a NCAA Division I Mideast Regional appearance. In his final college season, he struck out 145 batters in 118 innings. After signing with the A's, Beverlin spent only one week in Scottsdale before joining the Whitecaps.

Beverlin enjoyed the fact that he was able to play as a pro in his home state. "That does make it exciting," said Beverlin, whose hometown is just outside of Detroit. "A lot of my friends and family will get a chance to watch me. I think they're even more excited than I am."

Good-bye

For about four days, Marcel Galligani toiled on the bench, waiting impatiently to play. Nagging injuries and a low batting average began to hang a heavy load. His mind shifted to dismal possibilities.

"We were on the bus heading to Burlington," said pitcher Matt Walsh. "Chello sat behind me on the bus. I remember him saying that he was going to get released. I told him he was talking stupid."

On June 24 Galligani got three hits in a 7-5 tenth-inning loss to the Burlington Bees. But no matter how many pats on the back or how much praise he got from teammates, Galligani couldn't shed a feeling of loss.

"After the game he kept saying that this was it and he was going to get released," Walsh said. "Chello left our (hotel) room. Skip (manager Jim Colborn) called while he was away. When Chello returned, I told him that Skip called and wanted to talk with him. Chello said that this was it."

Fifteen minutes later, after midnight, Galligani returned and announced the news of his release. Word got around, and ten to fifteen players entered the room to console him. Later that night, as the news spread, somber Whitecaps players gathered in a Burlington sports bar to say farewell, one by one, to their former teammate. They were all in disbelief, all feeling sorry, all bleeding for a friend.

Even though he had gone three for four that night — ironically, the first time Galligani got three hits in a game all season — Galligani was released by Oakland. Hitting only .188, the organization said it was time for him to go.

"He wasn't going to get any playing time," explained Colborn. "We couldn't send him to Medford (lower Class A) because he'd already been there for two years. He needs to be challenged. It came a time where we didn't have the opportunity to give him. It's not a pleasant piece of news, but it cuts him free to go where he could be more productive with a job or with another team."

Breaking the news to Galligani wasn't one of the pleasures of being a manager. But someone had to do it. "My job is not only to do what's best for a guy's baseball career, but what's best for his life," said Colborn. "That gets into talking to them about their personal lives sometimes. It gets into talking about their personality and how they can grow up to become men. If a time comes in baseball where there's not an opportunity, then it's my job to tell them."

Colborn, always the optimist, viewed releasing a player as being in the best interest of everyone involved. With a low percentage of minor league players making it to the big leagues, it's an organization's duty not to waste anyone's time. "If it comes time where we're just using them for a Class A ball team, we're not doing our job," Colborn said.

In the 1960s, Colborn was himself a wide-eyed youngster making his bid in the minors, vying for a spot in the majors. He watched guys come and go, never believing he'd be next. "You have to stay positive," Colborn said. "You can't look over your shoulder. You have to remain focused. You must have that attitude. I never thought I'd get released. I always saw that as the other guy."

This time that other guy was a native New Yorker known to his teammates as "Chello." He was sorely missed. In honor of his roommate, Walsh scribbled Galligani's jersey number 8 on the back of his cap. Galligani also left Walsh his jersey pants. "That whole scene was weird, because it could've happened to any of us," Walsh said. "I didn't enjoy seeing my buddy crying. That whole incident made me scared."

With his release and plane ticket in hand, Galligani left Burlington for Grand Rapids, where he made the drive back to New York. "That was the longest drive of my life," said Galligani, who had joined the Whitecaps on April 23, moving up from extended spring training in Scottsdale after shortstop Jeff D'Amico was injured. "During the trip home I just thought what I was going to do."

Galligani eventually went back to Iona University to finish his degree in broadcasting. He planned on a possible comeback with another team.

Big George

No one had the explosive impact that George Williams brought to the Whitecaps when he arrived after the release of Marcel Galligani.

Hours after driving a U-Haul truck from Scottsdale to Burlington, Williams still had his foot on the gas in the Whitecaps' June 25 contest with the Bees. After making the two-day,

George Williams made his presence known while rehabbing with the Whitecaps. Courtesy the *Grand Rapids Press*.

1,600-mile drive, Williams went three for three, with a home run and three RBI's. A tenth-inning two-run homer by Vince LaChance off Zack Sawyer, however, gave Burlington a 7-5 victory before 2,221 fans at Community Field.

Williams, a switch-hitting catcher, joined the Whitecaps to get his right shoulder back into shape. He injured it playing winter ball in the Dominican Republic in 1993, and surgery followed in March 1994. "It hurts to throw, but I'm able to swing the bat without any pain," said Williams, who expected to be a designated hitter until the shoulder healed. "I started throwing for the first time a few days ago. I'm expected to rehab here for about a month."

While mending, the twenty-five-year-old Williams hoped to smash the ball the same way he did for Class AA Huntsville in 1993. He made the Southern League All-Star team that year with a .295 average, tenth best in the league. In 124 games he had twenty-six doubles, hit fourteen home runs, and drove in seventy-seven runs.

The Whitecaps were last in the league in hitting after the first half, so they craved Williams' offensive punch. "From now on, everyone will drive their cars on road trips, and they must drive all night," said a half-kidding Whitecaps manager Jim Colborn. "He's a much more sophisticated hitter than we're used to seeing here. You can tell by the way he takes pitches. He has a good, solid approach at the plate."

In the first inning, Williams singled in Jason McDonald for a 1-0 Whitecaps lead. Up 2-0 in the third with a runner on, Williams drove a shot over the right field wall to make the score 4-0.

The Bees kept chiseling away at the Whitecaps' lead until reliever Bill King gave up a solo homer that tied the score at 5-5 in the eighth. Sawyer relieved King in the ninth, and pitched well for two innings before allowing the winning shot by LaChance. The Whitecaps didn't help their cause by stranding thirteen runners on base.

Despite the loss, Williams was pleased that he was able to perform. "I didn't expect to play tonight," he said. "But since I arrived earlier than expected, I was put in. Besides the long drive, it was tough playing under the lights. I haven't done that in over a year. Once I got adjusted, everything went all right."

The Lacrosse, Wisconsin, native was taken by Oakland in the twenty-fourth round of the 1991 draft out of the University of Texas-Pan American. He played for Madison in 1992.

Williams is married to Chris, and they have two children, Erik, six, and Shelby, one. He said the travel can be tough on his family. "I'm sure it is, but they're used to it because we've traveled so much," Williams said.

◆   ◆   ◆

Williams did notice something strange when he first joined the Whitecaps. "I got off of the bus and went right into the clubhouse," he said. "I looked around and wondered where was my stuff. I had to go back outside to get my bags that were by the side of the bus. Then after the game, I had showered and was ready to leave. I noticed that my dirty uniform was still on the floor. I had to go put it in the laundry bags."

Welcome back to Class A baseball. The difference between Class A and other levels of baseball is more than degrees of talent. If Williams came off a bus in a Class AA town, he wouldn't have to carry his own bag. He would enter the clubhouse and find his belongings in place and his uniform on a hanger.

"Your shoes are polished every day," Williams said with a smile. "You take off your uniform, toss it on the floor, and the 'clubbies' (clubhouse workers) will pick it up and have it washed. If you forget something, they'll get it for you. Last year I broke my glove. A clubbie had a guy re-string it for me."

Then there are the food differences from Class A. Class A players eat so much peanut butter and jelly for pregame meals that it remains permanently on the roof of their mouths. The menu on the higher levels is a welcome change. "In some (Class AA) clubhouses on the road there would be juice machines, refrigerators with milk, and a meat platter," Williams said. "After games, you'd get fed meals like spaghetti dinners."

Whitecaps pitcher Scott Baldwin eagerly anticipated those days. "I'm definitely tired of peanut butter and jelly," Baldwin said. "Compared to what they (higher levels) eat, we must be on the low end of the totem pole."

Making sure the game goes smoothly are batboys (from left) Chris Walton, Sam Strater, Dave Lensink, and Matt Cinder.
Courtesy the *Grand Rapids Press*.

But the high end of that pole doesn't come without a price. The clubbies don't work for free. "The clubbies on the road are really good," Williams said. "Our clubbies at home would take care of us, but we didn't get a dinner like we did on the road. The clubbies on the road are the guys that you give tips, and they're the ones that have the (great) food for you. The clubbies for the home team do your laundry and get you some fruit."

Quad City

On June 26, the Whitecaps arrived in Quad City. It was the one-year anniversary of the flood that invaded John O'Donnell Stadium.

The Quad City stadium is adjacent to the Mississippi River. In 1993, floodwaters reached a depth of eight feet inside the park. The clubhouses and tunnels were completely submerged. As a result, the River Bandits had to postpone or cancel thirty games that year.

After the water receded in August 1993, repairs were quickly underway. The field had to be pulled up and completely replaced with new grass, and a new and improved drainage system was installed.

John O'Donnell Stadium has been the home of Quad City pro baseball since 1931. Originally named Municipal Stadium, the name was changed in 1970 in honor of a sports columnist for the *Davenport Times-Democrat*. A picturesque view of the Mississippi, with river boats and the Sentinel bridge in the foreground, makes it a favorite among Midwest League stadiums.

West Michigan's D. T. Cromer, who played here in 1993 with the Madison Muskies, enjoyed revisiting. "This is a good park," Cromer said. "It's been around for awhile. It has that old-school look. Plus, it's nice playing in a ball park where your dad once played."

Baseball Family

For more than twenty years, Roy and Donna Cromer have been on the run. Ever since the births of their minor league baseball sons — Tripp, twenty-six; Burke, twenty-four; David Thomas (D. T.), twenty-three; and Brandon, twenty — the Cromers have been true "gamers."

"We've seen over thirty different minor league parks since 1989 when Tripp was drafted," Roy Cromer said, while he and Donna visited Old Kent Park in August. "In 1992, we saw over 111 minor league, high school, and college games. We put forty-nine thousand miles on the car last year. We've driven close to four hundred thousand miles trying to see our boys play over the past few years."

Roy and Donna Cromer have been trying to keep up with their sons since the boys were growing up in Lake City and Lexington, South Carolina. While Dad was a high school baseball coach and junior varsity baseball coach at South Carolina University, the boys would play on the sidelines, dreaming of that one day when they would play in the majors.

D. T. Cromer steams toward home.   Courtesy the *Grand Rapids Press*.

That day has crept closer since three of the four were drafted. Tripp, a shortstop, was a third-round pick of the St. Louis Cardinals in 1989, and Burke signed as a free agent with the Atlanta Braves in 1992. D. T. was picked in the eleventh round in 1992 by the Oakland Athletics, and Brandon, a shortstop, went to the Toronto Blue Jays in the first round of the 1992 supplemental draft.

Brandon played for the Class A Hagerstown team in Maryland. Burke, a pitcher, suffered arm problems and quit after the 1993 season to become a golf pro in South Carolina.

Those times growing up with his siblings brought fond memories to the West Michigan outfielder. "We always played (baseball) when we were little," D. T. said. "But we played football and basketball just as hard. We also played tennis. We made state tournaments, and we played in tennis clubs. Baseball was always number one, but we played everything until we went to college."

D. T. emphasized that while he and his brothers played baseball, their father never put unwanted pressure on them. That might be hard to understand, since Roy himself has an impressive baseball bio. Roy played minor league ball from 1960-64 in the Cardinals organization, much of that time in the Midwest League. For twenty-three years he coached baseball on the high school and college levels. He's also a scout for several major league clubs.

But their father's background and love for the game never presented a problem for his sons. "He was more of a dad to us than a coach," D. T. said. "When he coached high school we would run around the park playing. If we did something wrong (playing baseball), he'd tell us, but he wasn't domineering. In our family, playing sports was an option. We didn't have to play if we didn't want to."

The pressure to play did come from older brother Tripp. Whatever he'd try, the others would follow. "D. T. learned to be such a competitor at an early age trying to keep up with his two older brothers," Roy said. "Tripp was the pacesetter. He set the tone."

Tripp gave the kind of direction that D. T. cherishes. "It helped learning from Tripp because he went through high school and college first," D. T. said. "That gave me a chance to see how he did things. The rest of us (brothers) always competed with each other, but we learned more from watching Tripp."

Tripp played his second season for Class AAA Louisville in 1994. He's the heir apparent to Cardinals' shortstop Ozzie Smith. Tripp credited his fortune of playing pro baseball to the household he grew up in. "At home, there was always someone to play with," he said. "Instead of staying in the house and playing video games, we'd be outside.

"Our dad didn't burn us out. Sometimes parents will make you do something and you rebel. My dad never made us play unless we wanted to."

The Cromer brothers never had to compete against each other in baseball while growing up. They all went to the same high school and South Carolina University, and even in Little League were usually on the same team. The only time they got to face each other was in other sports. "Tennis is the worst," D. T. said. "Tripp and Burke will always whip on me and Brandon in tennis and golf. Those are the only sports I'd get mad at them for beating me."

Most of the time the Cromer brothers have cheered each other on. D. T. was caught on several occasions reading *USA Today*, checking on scores from his brothers' games. The foursome kept in touch by telephone during the week. On off days, they would each try to visit the others.

And when the Cromer brothers couldn't visit, their parents would. "I wish they could be a little closer," Donna said. "They're really spread out (Michigan, Kentucky, and

Maryland; Burke played in Macon, Georgia). But the travel has given us a chance to meet some nice very nice people." And a chance to see the country.

Funny Bounces

For eight complete innings, West Michigan and Beloit took the 596 fans at Pohlman Field on a smooth ride to a tie score.

But two consecutive balks, followed by an ejection and a ground ball that froze an infielder in his tracks, ran the Whitecaps off course and eventually led to a 3-2 Brewers victory. The win inched Beloit closer to the first-place Whitecaps in the second-half Northern Division race. A victory by South Bend helped clutter the division.

Beloit manager Wayne Krenchicki liked his team's new position. "It's a two-game swing," Krenchicki pointed out. "We could've been three and a half out, instead we're one-half behind. The Whitecaps are playing with a lot of confidence right now, and this win helps change things in the minds of my players."

The Whitecaps wished for a change of mind by the umpires, especially in the final inning.

The ninth inning started simply enough. With the score tied, West Michigan's Jason Beverlin struck out the leadoff batter. Then Darrell Nicholas stepped to the plate. He was a prelude to chaos. Nicholas laid down a bunt between Beverlin and Vinny Francisco at second base. Francisco scooped up the roller and threw to first. Nicholas was called safe on a very close play.

Things heated up when base umpire Scott Bayley called a balk. Whitecaps manager Jim Colborn went out to discuss the matter, all in vain.

With first base open, Colborn signaled to intentionally walk Todd Dunn. After Beverlin's first wide toss, Bayley called another balk. Beverlin hopped off the mound. As Colborn sprinted onto the diamond, Bayley ejected Beverlin. Beverlin slammed the baseball to the ground before storming off the field.

"I didn't balk," explained Beverlin. "I threw over the first time, and I thought I did the same thing (motion) the second time. But I guess not. After the first balk, I was fine. I got ready for the intentional walk. I looked home, looked at second, and the next thing I know, I'm getting called for another balk."

While Beverlin was walking off, home plate umpire Steve Willard said something that got him excited. In came Brad Fischer, assistant director of player development. Fischer got Beverlin to leave, and then he had a small talk with Willard.

While this was going on, Colborn was still lecturing Bayley. Finally, order was restored and Jason Rajotte came in to replace Beverlin.

"It's a shame that they feel they have to call a balk when a guy is trying to walk someone intentionally," said Colborn. "That's got nothing to do with the game. He told me the rule is a rule, and I guess he has a point. I didn't think the first one was a balk. I was watching that. But he's the boss, and he's probably right. I just have to argue when that happens."

With Nicholas on third, the intentional walk was finally completed and Jonas Hamlin stepped to the plate. The Whitecaps hoped for either a ground ball for a double play or a grounder for a play at the plate. Instead, Hamlin hit a chopper to second. Francisco snared the ball on a hop, but couldn't make a play at first or at home. Instead, he held onto the ball and Nicholas scored the game winner.

"I was thinking too much of getting the runner at home instead of the double play," Francisco said. "By the time I thought of going for the double play, the runner had run past me and it was too late."

Even Hamlin was surprised that Francisco didn't go for the deuce. "He could've made a play on me," Hamlin said. "It was a high chopper — high enough so he couldn't make a play at home. Darrell (Nicholas) is really fast, and the play would've been real close at the plate."

Krenchicki was quite pleased with the victory, but he also thought it was a shame that a close game had to end with so much controversy. Still, he did agree with the calls. "They were balks," Krenchicki said. "He (Beverlin) didn't make a step or direction on the first one. It was unfortunate that a balk was called on the intentional walk. But that happened to us last year, and that's the rules."

◆ ◆ ◆

The following day, West Michigan lost another game in a chaotic affair. Behind a grand slam home run and another Whitecaps ejection, the Brewers chalked up their second win over the Whitecaps in as many days, this time 10-7 before 374 fans.

The loss by the Whitecaps, combined with a South Bend win over Cedar Rapids, tied those two teams at the top of the division. A win by Beloit brought the Brewers to just one-half game behind in second place.

For the second day in a row, the game was highlighted by an emotional inning. This time reliever Ryan Whitaker got the boot — and he didn't take it calmly. Whitaker relieved starter Gus Gil in the fourth inning, facing a 6-3 deficit with no outs. Beloit loaded the bases, and Jonas Hamlin launched a massive shot to center field for a grand slam home run. The blast gave the Brewers a 10-3 cushion.

"When the West Michigan pitchers are ahead in the count, they like to throw fastballs," said Hamlin, now with two grand slams for the season. "That particular pitcher (Whitaker) has done that to me before, and I was sitting fastball. He gave it to me, and I hit it."

After Hamlin's blast, Whitaker hit Brad Seitzer on the second pitch. Home plate umpire Scott Bayley ejected Whitaker for what he deemed as intentionally hitting the batter. Bayley had also ejected Beverlin the previous day.

Whitaker ran off the mound and got in Bayley's face. He had to be physically restrained by Whitecaps manager Jim Colborn. Whitaker finally calmed down and exited the field. "I didn't try to hit the guy," Whitaker said. "I could understand if I tried to hit the guy in the middle of the back or something, but I hit him on the inside elbow. If I could perfectly spot every pitch, every time, I wouldn't be in (Class) A ball."

The Whitecaps did collect seven runs in the effort, all scored with two outs. "The guys kept a good attitude and came back on them," Colborn said. "They certainly didn't give up. Our guys started banging the ball."

Fall from the Top

For the first time since June 28, West Michigan didn't sit atop the Northern Division. And for the eighth time in ten tries, the Whitecaps lost in extra innings — all thanks to the numbers put up by the Rockford Royals on July 13.

Behind an explosive five-run eleventh inning, the Royals defeated the Whitecaps 9-4 before 7,308 fans at Old Kent Park. The loss dropped the Whitecaps (13-8) to a second-place tie with Appleton (12-7). South Bend (14-7) took over the division lead with a win over Madison.

For Rockford (9-11), the first-half division winners, manager John Mizerock hoped the victory would change his team's fortune. "We haven't played well since the All-Star break," Mizerock said. "We haven't found anything to get us going. Maybe tonight we did. We'll see tomorrow."

Mizerock saw his team take a 2-1 lead in the second inning off a Jamie Byington single. Mat Reese's run-scoring double to left center tied the score for the Whitecaps at 2-2. In the fifth inning, with runners on first and third, George Williams jacked a single to score Juan Dilone, and the Whitecaps led 3-2.

For the next three innings, the Whitecaps cruised behind the pitching of starter Tim Kubinski and reliever Tim Bojan. Then Mike Sweeney's ninth-inning two-run blast gave Rockford a 4-3 edge. "We were just coasting along, getting ready to lose another one, and then that home run got us going," Mizerock said.

But the Whitecaps roared back in the bottom of ninth. Jason McDonald walked and stole second, and a walk to Dilone put runners on first and second. Reese attempted a bunt. The catcher Sweeney, seeing McDonald several feet off the bag, threw to second. The toss went wild into center field, and McDonald advanced to third.

Reese then grounded to second. The ball was scooped, but the throw to second was wild, and McDonald scored to tie the score at 4-4. "He does that on his own," said Whitecaps manager Jim Colborn, about McDonald forcing Sweeney to throw wild. "McDonald practically led us to a comeback in the ninth." Two strikeouts by Royals pitcher Nevin Brewer and a foul pop out ended the Whitecaps' threat.

In the eleventh Rockford loaded the bases, and Oscar Jimenez broke the game open with a two-run double to give Rockford a 6-4 lead. "I hit it well, and I knew it was a double," Jimenez said about his shot to the left field wall. "Hopefully, this can turn our slow second-half start around. We've played well. We just haven't got any breaks."

A two-run single and a delayed squeeze added three more Rockford runs before the inning ended. "We couldn't get over

Lawn seating is a popular venue for watching Whitecaps games.
Courtesy the *Grand Rapids Press*.

the hump," Colborn said. "We got close, but we couldn't quite punch it through."

◆ ◆ ◆

The following day, no matter how long West Michigan's Mat Reese stayed in the shower after the game, he still couldn't wash away the pain. That pain came from a 5-0 Rockford assault before 6,697 fans at Old Kent Park. The Whitecaps continued their plunge in the Northern Division race.

"I'm not happy at all," said Reese, emerging from the shower. "This team is a lot better than we've shown in the last four games. We have to just keep doing what we were doing in the first part of the second half and go with that. By no means are we going to give up. We're going to keep going, and good things are going to happen."

Four was definitely not West Michigan's lucky number. The Whitecaps now found themselves in fourth place, trailing Beloit, Appleton, and first-place South Bend. The loss was their fourth in a row, their longest losing streak since dropping five between May 31 and June 4. It was also their fourth shutout, the first since falling 2-0 to Fort Wayne on June 10.

Rockford, Northern Division winners in the first half of the season, had sunk to sixth place, but the last two wins began to show a better light. "Everyone's realizing that we need to come together like we were before," said Royals starter Toby Smith, who earned his first shutout with the victory. "Hopefully these wins will get us back on track."

The Royals' road back began with a team meeting. "Skip (manager John Mizerock) told us that we're almost at .500 ball, and we're not even playing our best," Rockford catcher Mike Sweeney said. "He told us to start picking things up. He said to make every at bat count, play hard, and the wins will take care of themselves."

That advice seemed to take hold for Rockford in the second inning. After loading the bases on Whitecaps starter Scott Baldwin, O. J. Rhone slammed a triple to right that put the Royals ahead 3-0. "It was a fastball," said Rhone about the pitch. "I was looking for something to put in play to drive in a run. I was fortunate that I was able to do that. Getting those runs helped us." So did a run in the third and a sacrifice fly in the fourth, giving Rockford a 5-0 tally.

Baldwin left after four innings with five hits, five runs, and five walks. He was followed in relief by Ryan Whitaker and Jason Beverlin. The duo allowed just one hit in five innings.

Pitching coach Gil Patterson acknowledged the relief effort. "They (Beverlin and Whitaker) kept their fastballs down, threw curveballs for strikes, changed speeds, and executed their game plan very well," Patterson said. "Baldwin didn't execute his quite as well, and that three-run triple with two outs hurt a little bit."

It didn't help that the Whitecaps couldn't get in position to score often enough.

♦ ♦ ♦

West Michigan briefly turned things around with the help of pitcher Derek Manning. Behind George Williams' solo homer and Manning's shutout pitching, they broke the four-game losing streak with a 2-0 victory over Rockford before 7,948 elated Old Kent Park fans.

In a game that took two hours and twenty minutes, the Whitecaps (14-9) collected their fifth shutout, the first since blanking South Bend on May 26. It was the first shutout for Manning, who won his second consecutive game in fine fashion.

Manager Jim Colborn enjoyed his team's return to the

win column. "This got us back to our normal game," Colborn said, "which is good pitching, get a run here and there, and good base running."

Colborn also had a good word for Manning. "Derek's looked very sharp in his last two outings. If he doesn't quit pitching like this, he won't get to stay here." A week earlier Manning allowed only four hits, two runs, and one walk while striking out seven in seven innings at Beloit. In the shutout against Rockford, the North Carolina graduate pitched seven complete innings, allowed five hits, struck out seven, and didn't permit a walk.

The only threat came in the first inning, with Rockford runners on first and third and one out. A pop out and a deep fly to David Keel at the right field wall put water on Rockford's fire.

Manning found it hard to explain his latest two performances. "It's weird when you're going good," he said. "I don't know if I'm in a zone, but when 'Orty' (catcher Randy Ortega) would give me a signal I wasn't thinking. I was just throwing to him and not thinking about the hitters. I threw a lot of fastballs inside early in the count. I was going to go away from that, but 'Orty' said since they weren't hitting me hard that we'd stick to the plan."

Ortega said Manning's command over his pitches made the difference in his last two outings. "He's definitely in a groove. He's fooling batters, and he's got them off balance. When a pitcher does that, it makes it tough on any batter to get a solid hit."

The Whitecaps got things going early when they manufactured their first run. In the first inning Vinny Francisco singled. On a ball four pitch to George Williams, Francisco darted for second. Rockford catcher Sal Fasano came out of his crouch to throw to second (although he didn't need to because it was ball four), and as he decided to hold back the ball slipped out and scooted between short and third. Francisco continued to run and was safe at third.

"The count was 3-1," Fasano said. "The ump's call was slower than usual, and I thought it was a strike since he delayed. So I came up throwing. Then he said ball, and I tried to hold up and it slipped out of my hand."

With Steve Cox at the plate, Williams broke for second and Fasano threw to Royals second baseman Jeremy Carr. Carr relayed to third as Francisco was halfway down the line. On the throw Francisco broke home. The throw from third baseman Lino Diaz hit Francisco in the back as he scored to put the Whitecaps ahead 1-0.

In the fourth Williams sent a fastball to the grassy knoll behind the right field wall, making the Whitecaps' lead 2-0. It was Williams' fourth homer in twenty games.

"We lost four in a row after starting off in first," Manning said. "Skip (Colborn) talked to us Friday night and said there's a long way to go. He said teams would give up — and he wanted to make sure we weren't one of them."

That Long Road Ahead

The start of the Whitecaps' longest road trip of the season (ten games) gave no clue to how it would finish.

In the road opener at Appleton, two heroes in unexpected roles stole the show. When it came to power, they were your kind of guys. When it came to driving in runs, spraying the ball all over the field, and throwing out runners from behind the plate, catchers Willie Morales and Randy Ortega were just what you ordered. But when it came to speed, well...

West Michigan was sparked in the second inning by two steals of home by unlikely base stealers Ortega and Morales, and went on to defeat the Foxes 14-4 behind fifteen hits at Goodland Field.

It was the sixth win in the last seven games for the Whitecaps as they chased first-place South Bend (20-8). The Silver Hawks maintained a half-game lead with a victory over Quad City, the tenth in their last eleven games.

The Whitecaps' attack began in the second inning. With the bases loaded on starter Shawn Estes, manager Jim Colborn sent Morales home from third. Morales slid in as the ball got by catcher Alex Sutherland. After Ortega went to third, Colborn signaled for him to steal too, and he beat the tag at the plate to give the Whitecaps a 2-1 lead. It was only the third stolen base of the season in four attempts by Morales, and Ortega's second in two attempts.

Morales now led the Whitecaps with eleven homers. He was second on the team with a .276 batting average and third with thirty-six RBI's. Ortega, a part-time player, was hitting .262 with twenty-seven RBI's.

"Basically, I'm in the lineup because of my speed," said Morales, holding back a smile. "I can't believe they (Appleton) weren't taking me seriously because of the threat I am."

Colborn wasn't surprised that the move caught Appleton off guard. Morales and Ortega were decoys for much of the season. "They've (other teams) seen a lot of our double steals, but those were merely camouflage to what our real trick play was, which is our quarter horses disguised as Clydesdales," said Colborn with a straight face. "We've been saving a little something extra for the end of the year."

Colborn took advantage of a slow delivery by pitcher Estes. The two consecutive steals of home unnerved third baseman Brian Wallace so he could barely move. "When he (Morales) went home, I was so surprised that I just froze," Wallace said. "I didn't hear anyone say anything. The second guy (Ortega) took off right in the middle of Estes' windup. I yelled that he was coming, but there wasn't a play."

Unfortunately, there wasn't much play left in the Whitecaps for the rest of the trip. They lost the next nine games.

The beginning of the end started with the celebration of four birthdays — David Keel, Mark Moore, Derek Manning, and radio announcer Rick Berkey. The birthdays are the only thing that was clear on exactly what happened at the Holiday Inn in Appleton. But whatever transpired, it affected the final nine games of the road trip.

No Vacancy

This series marked the last time the team would stay at the Holiday Inn in Appleton. The hotel terminated its contract with the Whitecaps based on unsubstantiated evidence of foul play. Rumors floated around the league about numerous incidents supposedly linked to Whitecaps players, who shared the hotel with several softball teams and other youth participating in a summer basketball tournament.

The hotel, one of the nicer places to stay in the league, also terminated its arrangements with every team in the Midwest League. Management from the hotel wasn't specific on the reason for the cancellations. "We're not taking any teams because we've had problems with all of them," said Jody

Schulz, manager of the Appleton Holiday Inn. "I don't want to throw stones and say anything (about the alleged incident). This is an upscale hotel, and we no longer want business from the (Midwest) League."

After talking with Schulz, Jim Colborn called his team together prior to the second night's game. "I was hurt by the allegations, and before checking with my players, I felt like they let me and the organization down," Colborn said. "(During the meeting) I got tears in my eyes. I didn't know what to do because I was so hurt. Before I could really speak I just walked out.

"That hotel incident knocked down our self worth. We lost the close games because the players felt like they let me and the organization down. They lost their self-esteem. When it came crunch time we couldn't do it anymore."

That insult came on top of injuries that punched so many holes in the Whitecaps' lineup it started to look like Swiss cheese.

Assisted by five Whitecaps errors, Appleton defeated the Whitecaps 7-2 in the second game of the series. The Whitecaps had committed eight errors in two games. "We got behind and tried to do too much by gambling, and that caused some errors," said Whitecaps manager Jim Colborn. "I'd like to give some guys some rest. But I don't know if I can. Maybe I'll hope for a rainout."

Water couldn't heal the injuries to D. T. Cromer, Mat Reese, or Tony Banks. Several of the Whitecaps were out of their regular positions during the game. First baseman Steve Cox was forced to play right field, Jason McDonald (second baseman) played shortstop and center field, and catcher Mark Moore was at first base.

In the third game, two West Michigan errors quickly led to Appleton runs. With two outs and the Foxes leading 1-0, shortstop Fred Soriano booted a slow roller, a play he could usually make blindfolded. Starter Gus Gil walked the next two batters, and James Clifford, who entered the game two for twenty-five, slammed a single to put Appleton up 3-0.

In the third inning errors again hurt the Whitecaps. After West Michigan cut the deficit to 3-2, Appleton's Jason Cook singled to center. Raul Ibanez took off from first, rounded second, and slid into third in front of a wild throw from center field. Gil backed up the play, but his throw to second, to get Ibanez out going for the bag, was also wild and Cook scored to make it 4-2.

Clifford struck the Whitecaps again, taking Gil's pitch over the right field wall for a 6-2 Foxes' win.

In the final game against Appleton, Midwest League All-Star pitcher Scott Baldwin couldn't even resemble an all-state player. The Whitecaps left-hander had a performance that he would just as soon lose in the statistical file. Five first-inning walks and three wild pitches helped the Foxes to a 14-2 victory on a sunny Sunday July 24 afternoon at Goodland Field. It was the most runs given up by the Whitecaps since losing 17-3 at Clinton on May 8.

Baldwin started the game by walking the first two batters. He got Mike Barger to fly out before allowing a single that scored the Foxes' first run. Then the bottom fell out for the Whitecaps. A wild pitch in the dirt scored a run, followed by a walk. Another wild pitch made the score 3-0. Two consecutive walks followed to load the bases before Baldwin threw his third wild pitch of the inning, bringing in a fourth Appleton run.

In the second inning, Baldwin walked his sixth batter, bringing Colborn and trainer Brian Thorson to the mound. Baldwin left the game as Tim Bojan came in relief. "My arm was just dead," said Baldwin, who lost his third game in a row. "I didn't have anything on it, and I didn't know where the ball was going. It was like I ran in a marathon and went

141

Fred Soriano shows sure hands at shortstop.
Courtesy the *Grand Rapids Press*.

swimming before the game. It just wasn't there. It just felt like I was throwing with an ankle weight on my wrist. This happened to me before in college. I just took a little rest, and I was fine."

Putting Bojan on the mound didn't matter to Appleton. The Foxes slammed nine runs in the third inning. The scoring was capped by Fred McNair's massive blast over the center field wall, four hundred feet away. The Foxes led 13-0 after three.

The loss dropped the Whitecaps (19-13) three and one-half games behind first-place South Bend (22-9), who defeated Quad City in extra innings. Appleton (17-13) remained in third place four and one-half games out.

Throughout the four-game series the Whitecaps committed eleven errors and left thirty-eight runners on base. Those numbers were largely the result of injuries to players in key positions.

West Michigan manager Jim Colborn didn't have the luxury of giving players needed rest because he didn't have anyone to replace them in the lineup. "Once everyone is healthy, we'll get the big wave machine rolling again and reel off some victories," Colborn hoped. "When we get 'Big Screen' (injured outfielder Mat Reese) back in there, we'll be able to take on the double A team."

The Ball Keeps Rolling

After losing two at Kane County, the Whitecaps' dismal road trip continued to Rockford. The opener there was a game manager Jim Colborn would just as soon hide under the carpet. But Colborn didn't want any alibis, and he tossed aside all excuses. The West Michigan manager took total blame for the Whitecaps' 8-7 loss in thirteen innings to the Royals at Marinelli Field.

The sixth consecutive loss dropped the Whitecaps (19-16) to fourth place, four games behind idle South Bend (22-11). Second-place Rockford (21-14) had won eleven straight games and was two games out.

West Michigan missed a chance at gaining a half game while leading 6-3 in the eighth inning. Rockford loaded the bases on reliever Jason Rajotte, so Colborn called for pitcher Zack Sawyer. After watching several warmup tosses, plate umpire Steve Willard went out to the mound and was joined by Colborn. That's when Willard notified the Whitecaps manager that Sawyer couldn't pitch because he wasn't on the lineup card.

"He (Willard) came out and said that he had some bad news for me," Sawyer said. "He said that I couldn't pitch because Jim (Colborn) forgot to put me on the scorecard. I've never been in that situation before. I thought that the umpire and both managers could clear it up. I didn't realize that it was a rule, and that I couldn't pitch. I was a little ticked off, because I wanted to save those runs."

When the managers meet with the umpires prior to the game, they give the umpires a list of players available to play. Colborn mistakenly wrote down Scott Baldwin's name twice, as number 30 and number 37 (Sawyer's number). Midwest League rules state that no player can participate unless he's listed on the lineup card as a starter or substitute.

"It was a major mess-up by me," Colborn said. "I had flashbacks of managers coming to the mound and taking the ball away from me when I was a (major league) pitcher. The humiliation of failure when you let the team down as a pitcher resurfaced today when I let the team down by not putting a player on the lineup card. I take the blame. It was my screw-up. I guess I'm going to make mistakes. I hope it won't happen again."

Ryan Whitaker was Colborn's new choice. Rockford jumped all over Whitaker, scoring four runs in the eighth inning to take a 7-6 lead. But the Whitecaps came back to tie the score at 7-7 in the ninth on a two-out single by Steve Cox that drove in Fred Soriano from second. A renewed effort on the mound by Whitaker and two fine defensive plays by Juan Dilone in left field and Cox in right forced the game into extra innings.

Tim Bojan kept the score knotted in the late going. But in the thirteenth, outfielder/infielder Jason McDonald was called to the mound because no other pitcher was available. A bases-loaded single scored the winning run.

Rockford manager John Mizerock pointed to Colborn's lineup mistake as the turning point for his team. "Obviously that was key," Mizerock said. "I'm sure they'd rather have had Sawyer pitching instead of McDonald. It was a mistake, and we took advantage of it."

◆ ◆ ◆

The following day, the losing streak went so deep that all West Michigan could do was throw things in despair. Not even an emotional outburst by George Williams could prevent the slide as the Whitecaps lost for the eighth consecutive time in a 5-4 thriller at Rockford. It was the team's third consecutive one-run loss.

The Whitecaps (19-18) remained in fourth place, but Rockford (23-14), riding high on a thirteen-game winning streak, tied South Bend (22-13) for first.

For the third time in this series, the Whitecaps took an early lead. But just like before, they could only watch helplessly as the Royals came back for another victory.

The string of losses had the Whitecaps confused. "We're still battling. It's just bad luck," said starter Bill King. "We hang in there, and we get into a good situation to win, but midway in the game things don't go our way. It's become real frustrating. You play a team close like this, who's won thirteen in a row, and you wonder what it takes to get a win. We've looked strong. It's always just one little thing that makes things not go our way."

With the score tied 2-2, things didn't go Williams' way in the eighth inning when home plate umpire Steve Willard called him out on a third strike. While arguing the call, Williams dropped his bat and helmet at the plate, and then Willard tossed him out. But before Williams left, he had to be physically restrained by manager Jim Colborn. Before finally going to the showers, Williams tossed a chair and a garbage can onto the field.

The outburst inspired Rockford. In the top of the ninth Whitecaps reliever Jason Rajotte was greeted with a double. A grounder moved Braxton Hickman to third, and Sal Fasano singled to center for Rockford's 4-2 lead. The Royals ended the inning with a 5-2 margin.

The Whitecaps cut the deficit to 5-4 on a two-run homer by Steve Cox in the top of the ninth, but that's all the Whitecaps had left.

Rockford was fast approaching the Midwest League record of seventeen consecutive wins, accomplished by Cedar Rapids in 1965. But the Royals' streak would halt at fifteen games.

The Return

It was great for West Michigan to be back home in Old Kent Park, snapping the losing streak with a victory over Appleton in a brief, two-game homestand. Days later it was another homecoming of sorts when the Whitecaps visited Madison the first weekend of August.

West Michigan trainer Brian Thorson pointed out his condominium as the team bus rolled by.

George Williams and his son Erik were greeted by several fans yelling out their names.

Zack Sawyer had to take a stroll around Warner Park to take it all in. And a smile creased Vinny Francisco's face as he walked out of the clubhouse.

Seven Whitecaps played for the Madison Muskies before the Oakland Athletics moved the franchise to West Michigan for the 1994 season. Six Whitecaps played in Madison in 1993. Williams played for the Muskies in 1992.

Playing for Madison and returning after one season was like coming home. "It seems like I've only been gone for a few weeks," Sawyer said. "We drove past where our apartments were, and everything was painted red when it used to be green. It's nice to be back. And it was weird dressing in the visitors clubhouse."

Francisco, who honeymooned in Madison in 1993, was pleased with the changes at the stadium. "Everything looks so much better," said Francisco, who spent two seasons here. "I consider this my (American) hometown."

Williams, from Lacrosse, Wisconsin, was impressed with the pleasant greetings he received from several fans before the August 5 game. "It feels good when you come back to a place after two years and you're remembered," Williams said. "But some fans remember Erik more than they remember me."

One fan especially remembered Brian Eldridge. "He used to be my bowling partner," said long-time Madison fan Lorina Buechner. "I miss all of the players (former Muskies). They'll always be a part of this town."

Whitecaps who were formerly Muskies included D. T.

Cromer, Tim Bojan, Mark Moore, Eldridge, Sawyer, Williams, Francisco, trainer "Doc" Thorson, and pitching coach Gil Patterson.

While the Whitecaps became reacquainted with their former home park, the current team, the Cardinals, were themselves planning to leave Madison for Battle Creek, Michigan, where they'll play in the 1995 season.

The prime reason Oakland moved its Class A team from Madison to West Michigan was the need for ballpark improvements. Fans, players, and affiliates have all wanted a new stadium with modern amenities, but that didn't happen and now the Cardinals will move.

Final Lap

The Whitecaps' season spiraled down to the final ten regular season games. Fortunately, those games were scheduled for the pleasant confines of Old Kent Park. Not only did the Whitecaps still have a shot at making the playoffs, but added to the mix was the chance to break the Class A all-time attendance record (463,039) set by Denver in 1949. That would take an average crowd of 6,800 fans for the ten home dates.

West Michigan general manager Scott Lane was easy to spot those days. He was in a party mood, with a smile that stretched from Interstate 131 North to 131 South. "It's a cherry on top," said Lane about the possibilities. "This is beautiful. The fans deserve the attendance record and a postseason. Making the playoffs is a fairy tale. I'd love for us to go all the way."

Of the seven teams in the Northern Division, the Whitecaps were in the driver's seat with all their remaining games at home. They were 35-25 at Old Kent Park and 31-37 on the road. West Michigan (32-28) was one game behind second-place Beloit (33-27) and five and one-half behind first-place Rockford.

The Whitecaps had two chances to make the playoffs. Rockford won the division in the first half and would host the first playoff game on September 4. If Rockford also won the division in the second half, the second-place team would make the playoffs. If Rockford fell out of first, than the new first-place team would play Rockford.

The stage was set. The Whitecaps were ready to play. The team believed the fans would help make the difference.

The crowd is always a plus at Old Kent Park.
Courtesy the *Grand Rapids Press*.

"I always play better at home," Steve Cox said. "The crowd is a big plus. This homestand is going to be fun, because this is the first time all year we've really been in a race. This is going to be exciting for the fans and the players."

D. T. Cromer, who played at often-empty Madison Warner Park as a Muskie in 1993, got an extra jolt at Old Kent Park. "Large crowds make it more exciting," Cromer said. "In Madison you had to go out and play for yourself and have the desire to play the game. If you're down (emotionally) at Old Kent Park, you have the fans to bring you up."

No matter how big a boost the players received from the fans over the next few days, outfielder Mat Reese said it still came down to the players picking each other up. "We're playing good ball right now," Reese said. "The pitchers are doing well, and the hitting is coming around. If we continue to do that we have a chance."

West Michigan manager Jim Colborn liked his chances so much that he made a promise. "We're going to show our fans the most exciting baseball of the year," said Colborn. "We're going to get involved with the fans' excitement, and we're going to bring a championship to West Michigan."

Colborn was at least half right. The most exciting games at Old Kent Park came during those last two weeks in August. The gut-busting, highlight-film, explosive baseball began with the very first game.

Fort Wayne first baseman Chad Rupp wanted to take this one over. He knew his miss had the potential to follow him in his sleep. Rupp's dropped foul ball for an error in the fourth inning led to a tie score and kick-started West Michigan toward a 6-4 victory. Despite its last place position, Fort Wayne (29-32) still had a chance, and Rupp hoped he hadn't let one slip away.

The Wizards led 3-2 midway through the fourth inning. With one out and Juan Dilone on second, Eric Martins popped up in foul territory. Rupp got under the ball and made a step back, but the ball bounced off his glove as he fell to the ground. Martins took advantage and smacked a liner down third for an RBI double and a 3-3 score.

"It's disappointing, because it was the second out of the inning," said Rupp, who had beat the Whitecaps with a ninth-inning three-run homer the week before in Fort Wayne. "If I would've got the out, it could've changed the momentum in our favor."

This time, though, the pendulum swung to the Whitecaps' side. "I was glad to get the second chance," Martins said about the dropped foul ball. "I felt good going up to the plate, and I was mad at myself for swinging at that pitch (that he fouled off). I'm happy he dropped it."

Jim Colborn wasn't surprised that his team took advantage of a mistake, but he wasn't pleased with leaving fourteen runners on base. "This is an opportunistic team," the Whitecaps manager said, "but I'm surprised we didn't score more with that many hits."

Fort Wayne broke a 1-1 tie to move ahead 3-1 in the third. That same inning the Wizards put runners on first and second with no outs. After a brief meeting with pitching coach Gil Patterson, West Michigan starter Tim Kubinski settled in and got himself out of the jam on a line drive for a double play. The inning ended when a runner was caught stealing.

"I don't know what was going on early," said Kubinski, who gave up seven hits and three earned runs. "They hit my mistakes. I didn't pitch differently late in the game. They just didn't hit me as hard. I was getting killed out there. But it helps your confidence when your team keeps coming up with runs."

Those runs kept coming even after the Whitecaps tied the score. Dilone continued the batting practice display, driving in two runs with a single in the fifth for a 5-3 lead.

The Whitecaps collected sixteen hits, with four batters knocking three hits each. Still, the Whitecaps (33-28) remained five and one-half games out of first and one game behind second-place Beloit, who defeated Burlington 5-4.

◆ ◆ ◆

Dilone, who recently snapped out of a slump, got into the excitement of a potential postseason. "We're playing very well, and we're looking for the playoffs," Dilone said. "We're playing good together. Everyone is doing a good job at his position and at the plate. That's what we'll have to do if we want to win it."

The Whitecaps won their fourth straight game with the help of Dilone's bat. Dilone's dramatic twelfth-inning solo homer gave the Whitecaps a 5-4 victory over the Kane County Cougars in the third game of the ten-game homestand. That dramatic finish was the highlight of the final regular homestand, and the win helped West Michigan (35-28) keep pace, one-half game behind second-place Beloit.

West Michigan manager Jim Colborn couldn't keep his emotions in check. When Dilone took the ball deep into the night sky and over the wall, an elated Colborn stood erect in the third base box with his arms extended in the air. The playoff race had taken control. "This was the greatest game of the year," Colborn said. "You can trace Dilone's hot streaks with the team's winning streaks. He can carry a team with his base running, with his defense, and with his hitting."

The game almost ended in the ninth inning when Dilone bopped one to deep left field. Fort Wayne's Billy McMillon made a fine catch with his back to the wall to prevent it from going out.

"That guy made a great catch in left field," said Dilone, who was second in homers for the Whitcaps with eleven. "I thought that ball was out of the ball park. When I hit the second one (in the twelfth), I just watched it as I ran the bases. It had good height, and it got out of here. Hitting a homer to win a game is a dream. I feel good about it. And I feel good about the way we've been playing."

The good feelings continued when West Michigan drew a season-high 8,200 fans on August 27. The Whitecaps also won their fifth game in a row. The latest win set up the most important series of the year — a four-game matchup with Beloit that could determine which of the two teams made the playoffs.

"I get chills just thinking about it," said Mat Reese. "The stage is set. Both teams are in position, and everyone will be up. It could come down to the last at-bat on who wins the series."

The opener with Beloit came down to one final play. Here was Reese's chance. The game was on the line, and the manager of the major league club was in attendance.

Big Screen

They called Reese "Big Screen" because he played as if he was on television. But a throw to the plate that nailed Reese nearly cancelled West Michigan's show.

The Whitecaps fell to the Beloit Brewers 3-2 before 8,145 fans at Old Kent Park. Oakland Athletics manager Tony La Russa was among the crowd.

It was the first loss in six games for West Michigan, but

Mat "Big Screen" Reese hits one for the highlight films.
Courtesy the *Grand Rapids Press*.

more importantly, the Whitecaps slipped one and one-half games behind second-place Beloit in the final charge for a playoff spot. West Michigan (36-29) had three games left with Beloit (37-27) in this crucial series.

Despite the loss, Reese (who went four for four), still liked West Michigan's chances. "We have to continue what we've been doing," Reese said. "We have to continue playing hard. We control our own destiny. We're going to battle to the end, and Beloit knows that."

Beloit also knew that Reese would try to score on a hit. Down by a run in the ninth, Reese led off the inning with a single. Vinny Francisco hit a soft liner that was misplayed by Brewer center fielder Darrell Nicholas. But when the ball scooted away as Reese rounded third, left fielder Michael Dumas backed up the play. Dumas threw to shortstop Danny Klassen, and Klassen threw a strike home. Reese slid head-first, but catcher Glenn Sutko blocked the plate and made the tag.

"I saw him coming all the way," Sutko said about Reese. "His legs got weary, because he slowed up going to third. He slid wide at the back part of the plate, but he couldn't get the plate because my foot was there. It looked close because he was there before the ball, but I told the umpire before the play to get a good look because I was blocking the plate."

Manager Jim Colborn, who waved Reese home, didn't hesitate with his decision. "I saw the play clearly, and I made my judgment," Colborn said. "It was the right judgment, and I had to take a chance right there.

"Being behind a game-and-a-half doesn't really matter. Our backs are against the wall, and we just have to win the rest of them."

Reese's nickname goes back to last season at Southern Oregon. "Mat always plays like he's on television," said pitcher Derek Manning, trying to describe Reese's confident style. "Last year in Southern Oregon one of our players said that Mat plays like he's on a big screen TV." And the name has been with Reese ever since.

"It was all in fun," said Reese about the nickname. "I like it. It stuck, and everyone calls me that."

Reese almost got called something else during a game in Spokane, Washington, for Southern Oregon in 1993. Down 2-1 in the middle innings, Reese stepped to the plate and nailed a high fly ball to right center. "The sun was going down so you couldn't really see the ball," Reese said. "I did see the two outfielders come together at the wall, but I didn't see anyone make the catch. I saw the umpire put his hand up, and I thought he signaled for a home run."

Visibility in the outfield was difficult because of the setting sun, the misty air, and the fact that the outfield wall was white like the ball. So when the ball left his sight, Reese started his stroll. "I looked at the umpire, and I thought he was signaling that I hit a home run, so I started trotting around second," Reese said. "I noticed something kind of odd. As I rounded third, our manager, Dick Scott, didn't shake my hand."

Whitecaps catcher Mark Moore was also on that team that memorable night. He remembered Scott holding his hands up, trying to tell Reese to hold up. Reese also got confused when the Southern Oregon bench was praising him for how hard he juiced the ball. "Reese was pumped," Moore said. "It was so funny. If he would've got to third and walked off of the field, he would've been fine. But he made that left turn."

Wrong move. While Reese was rounding third, the Spokane infield was throwing the ball around. The Southern Oregon bench was in stitches. "By the time he gets home, I'm laying on my side, and the bench is laughing so hard," Moore said.

What Reese didn't realize is that his fly ball was caught

at the wall. He never noticed the catch or the umpire ruling it an out. "When I got home, the umpire told me I was out," Reese said. "So I walk back to the dugout, and the fans are laughing. I have a big (embarrassing) smile on my face. The whole thing was so ridiculous."

That wasn't the end of Reese's twilight zone day. In his next at bat, he disagreed with two called strikes. After grounding out, Reese had a few undisclosed words for the umpire. He was immediately tossed from the game.

Second Gear

This Whitecaps magic began to take a grip on West Michigan's playoff run. Time and time again, the Whitecaps came from behind in the late innings thanks to timely hitting, clutch pitching, and a little hocus-pocus.

A bases-loaded wild pitch and an RBI single by Eric Martins in the ninth led to a 6-5 Whitecaps' victory over Beloit before 7,906 on August 29. It was the first time Old Kent Park had drawn under 8,000 since August 10. West Michigan was 12,373 fans short of setting a new Class A record.

It was the fourth time in the last five games that the Whitecaps won a game in their final at-bat. The victory also inched West Michigan (37-29) to one-half game behind Beloit (37-28) in the race for the final playoff spot.

Jim Colborn liked the position his team had put itself in. He also enjoyed the dramatic finishes. "Before I went to the coach's box in the ninth inning, I had my arms raised in the

West Michigan fans fill Old Kent Park to break a 45-year-old Class A attendance record. Courtesy the *Grand Rapids Press*.

air," the manager said. "I had a feeling we'd win. If these guys are close at the end (of the game), I wouldn't want to be the other team. We have an incredible ability to come from behind. This is unbelievable."

That's how the Brewers felt at the end. Leading 5-4 in the ninth, Beloit put runners on first and third with one out. West Michigan's Tim Bojan came in relief and notched three straight strikeouts to get his team out of the jam.

"That just set the tone, and it gave us the momentum we needed," Colborn said.

That momentum carried over to the bottom of the ninth and continued to carry as West Michigan loaded the bases with one out. The magic began when a wild pitch got past catcher Glenn Sutko, scoring Fred Soriano from third to tie the game. The rally continued with Martins at the plate.

"I went up to the plate with swinging on my mind," Martins said. "But Skip called me to the side and asked me if I wanted to lay down a bunt. That kind of surprised me, but I figured I might as well swing. Skip goes with a player's instinct. He allowed me to make the decision to hit."

Hit indeed. Martins punched a single to right field, and the winning run crossed the plate.

"This win turns the momentum back to our side," Martins said. "We've got two more games in our back yard, and they (Beloit) know now that we won't quit. They may come out a little hesitant, because we're not going to lay down. Yesterday's win was big for them. Today's is even bigger for us."

After sitting out a day because of a rain delay, the Whitecaps and Brewers resumed action on August 31. The Whitecaps' sweep of the Brewers in the doubleheader and the 8,193 fans at Old Kent Park set the stage for capturing a new Class A attendance record and a berth in the playoffs. The Whitecaps didn't have to wait long.

Playoff Bound

The West Michigan clubhouse resembled chaos on September 1. Players doused each other with beverages. Laughter bounced off the walls. High fives and back slaps were shared throughout the room.

The cause for celebration was West Michigan's 8-2 victory over Fort Wayne that bumped the Whitecaps into the divisional playoffs.

Also, the Whitecaps set a new Class A season attendance record. The crowd of 8,168 pushed West Michigan to 471,207, beating Denver's record which had held since 1949.

♦ ♦ ♦

The next day's game with Fort Wayne would be the regular season finale.

While his players enjoyed the moment, manager Jim Colborn observed from a distance. "This is very satisfying," said a beer-drenched Colborn. "We felt like we were going to do it. Playing these last ten games at home saved us."

Colborn was quick to share the credit. "If anything was accomplished, it was with the attitude that it's not me (Colborn) doing it. It was the players. Actually, it was a group thing. We all did our share."

David Keel, whose time had been limited because of an injured hand, did his part in the playoff clincher with a homer, triple, and three RBI's. "I've been out for close to a month," Keel said. "It takes a little while to get a groove back. I've never felt as comfortable as I did tonight. It came at a good time."

Brian Eldridge figured it was about time for his career. "This is the first time since I've signed (with the Athletics organization in 1992) that I've been on a team in the playoffs," said Eldridge, who was moved to West Michigan on July 10 from Modesto, also playoff bound. "I'm really excited about the postseason. We're focused, and we're going to give it our best."

Starter Matt Walsh gave it his all against Fort Wayne. He gave up only four hits in five innings pitched, allowing one earned run and striking out six.

Pitcher Bill King douses teammate Matt Walsh after the Whitecaps clinched a playoff berth with an 8-2 win over Fort Wayne.
Courtesy the *Grand Rapids Press.*

Just like the Whitecaps pitchers the night before, Walsh was fueled by the fans' frenzy. "The crowd was into it," Walsh said. "That was the biggest crowd I've pitched in front of, and it was the biggest start of my career. I became a little nervous at the beginning, but I finally settled down."

Postseason

Despite all the glory and excitement the Whitecaps had experienced during their first season, there was one thing they wanted to forget — their last regular season visit to Rockford.

But a hard run into the playoffs brought them back to Marinelli Field. Rockford manager John Mizerock saw the storm rolling in. "They're playing better than the last time we played them," Mizerock said. "I hope they cool off. A different guy comes through for them every night."

Both teams hoped for someone to come through for them over the next three days as the Whitecaps and the Royals opened the first game of the best-of-three Northern Division playoffs September 4. The winner would advance to the Midwest League best-of-five championship series against the winner of the Southern Division playoffs between Springfield and Cedar Rapids.

Rockford earned their playoff berth by winning the first half of the season with a 44-25 record. For the full season they finished at 89-50, best in the league. Despite their sixth-place standing in the first half, West Michigan came on strong at the end, winning twelve of their last fifteen games to finish with a 40-30 second-half record, 74-65 for the season.

Rockford breezed through each half of the 140-game season. West Michigan manager Jim Colborn said they were clearly the best in the Midwest League. "They've proven that with their record, their (individual) statistics, and by their all-stars," Colborn said. "By any standard they've proven that they're the best team in the league, except for one last standard — the divisional playoffs. That's where we step in."

Before the Whitecaps could step in, they wanted to erase the memory of that last visit to Rockford. The low point of a miserable 1-9 road trip, the Whitecaps lost all four games to the Royals by one run. The series was further marred by the ejection of George Williams and Colborn's failure to list pitcher Zack Sawyer on his lineup card, costing the team a needed reliever and probably the game.

"We did that to get them overconfident," Colborn said about the unfortunate circumstances. "Now they'll think they're playing some bumbling idiots."

Fat chance. West Michigan was 6-8 against Rockford in the regular season, and five of those games were decided by one run.

◆ ◆ ◆

The Royals were no slouches either. They were led by Carlos Mendez, who won the league batting title with a .355 average. He did even better against the Whitecaps, with a .394 average in ten games.

Rockford's top pitchers included Phil Grundy (15-8, 3.21 ERA) and Kenny Ray (10-4, 1.82 ERA), who was slated to start the playoff series. Ray was 1-1 against West Michigan during the regular season.

One factor that worried the Royals in the postseason was the absence of Sal Fasano, who led the team in homers and RBIs. Fasano was moved up to Wilmington several weeks prior to the playoffs.

Even without Fasano, West Michigan playoff-opening pitcher Tim Kubinski still respected the Royals' attack. "The heart of their lineup is the 2-3-4-5 spot," said Kubinski, who was 1-1 against Rockford. "(Mike) Sweeney, (Lino) Diaz, and Mendez are three tough hitters. If you can contain those three you have a chance."

For their part, Rockford wanted to contain the West Michigan bats, but several Whitecaps had given the Royals fits. D. T. Cromer and George Williams slammed Royals'

163

pitching. Cromer had eight hits in twenty-three at-bats against Rockford. Williams had ten hits in twenty-nine at-bats, including two home runs and five RBI's.

♦ ♦ ♦

All of that was history. Everything West Michigan put together during the final ten-game homestand to capture a playoff berth was gone. The exciting action and vigor that won twelve of their last fifteen regular season games evaporated. Against Rockford in the playoffs the clutch hitting vanished. The superb defense was nowhere to be found, and what there was didn't come close to making a fantastic finish.

This was all too obvious in the Whitecaps' opener in the Northern Division playoffs. West Michigan errors and clutch hitting by Rockford combined to give the Royals a 7-0 victory over the Whitecaps before 1,031 fans (about 200 from West Michigan) at Marinelli Field.

Three Whitecaps errors contributed to two Rockford runs, and twice West Michigan left two men on third with one out. It wasn't the kind of baseball seen from the Whitecaps lately.

"No kidding," said manager Jim Colborn. "Not only did they beat us, but we beat ourselves. We came out tight in the first inning. After that we played OK, but not with the intensity that we've played with before. I don't know. I'm a little puzzled. It'll be different tomorrow."

Rockford walked and singled to begin the first inning. Carlos Mendez, who led the league in hitting, smashed a grounder through the legs of shortstop Fred Soriano to score the game's first run. Mendez was thrown out trying to stretch the hit to second.

The Royals then went to their bag of tricks. Mike Sweeney, who had singled, took off for second, and the throw from catcher Willie Morales was cut off by second baseman Eric Martins when Jimmie Byington headed home from third. Martins' throw home was high, forcing Morales to come up the third base line a few feet. Byington slid under the glove, and Rockford led 2-0.

"The error and the runs we scored in the first put the pressure on them," said Rockford manager John Mizerock. "We scored more runs, and the pitching by (Ken) Ray made it tough for them to come back."

West Michigan's first attempt at a comeback came on Soriano's shot over the left fielder to begin the sixth inning. Soriano was called out going to third, but the call was changed because Soriano had been blocked on the base path by the first baseman. The opportunity was stalled when a strikeout and groundout ended the inning.

West Michigan starter Tim Kubinski settled in from an unfortunate first inning and held off Rockford until the sixth. Then the Royals loaded the bases and jumped ahead 4-0 on a single and groundout. Kubinski was replaced by Al Gogolin. Two walks scored another Rockford run before a fielder's choice and strikeout by Mendez with the bases loaded ended the rally.

Ray continued to baffle the Whitecaps in the seventh when for the second consecutive inning a runner was left stranded on third. Ray pitched seven shutout innings, allowing one walk and striking out five.

"Winning the first game is big, because it puts us up in a short series," Mizerock said. "We're going to try to win the next game. We don't want to string this along."

The Party's Over

West Michigan's David Keel never danced around with his answers, and his tune remained on key after the Whitecaps' loss on Labor Day, September 5. "We ran into Rockford," Keel said. "They're a good team. They did what it takes to win, and we didn't. We poured it on for so long just to get into the playoffs. It became hard to keep that going. Losing the first game at their place didn't help."

Playing before 8,077 fans at Old Kent Park, the Whitecaps watched an early two-run lead vanish as Rockford went on to a 6-3 victory and a sweep of the best-of-three Northern Division playoff series.

The Royals moved on to the Midwest League best-of-five title series against Cedar Rapids, the second-half winner in the Southern Division and the eventual MWL champions.

The Whitecaps' season now ended. They would have plenty of time to reflect on an exciting year. The offseason would also leave the team wondering what happened with so much promise late in the season.

"We may have relaxed (in the playoffs) after the (twelve-of-fifteen) streak that got us here, because I just didn't see the focus," West Michigan manager Jim Colborn said. "I only saw the focus here and there instead of for nine innings. I hope we learned something from that.

"It's been a successful season nevertheless. We accomplished more than anyone expected, but it's still a disappointment that we didn't win a playoff game when we were capable."

After being shut out in game one, the Whitecaps were capable of coming from behind in game two. West Michigan tied the score in the first inning at 1-1 on George Williams' ground-rule double. A wild pitch scored Brian Eldridge from third, and a sacrifice fly by Mark Moore gave the Whitecaps a 3-1 lead.

Starter Derek Manning held off Rockford until the torrid third inning. With the bases loaded, a single, fielder's choice, and single to center put Rockford ahead 5-3.

An RBI single off reliever Tim Bojan in the fifth extended the Royal's lead. Rockford starter Phil Grundy (who beat the Whitecaps for the first time after having lost three straight) and his relief corps held West Michigan at bay, but not without controversy.

Things heated up when Juan Dilone argued a called third strike with home plate umpire Mark Carlson in the seventh. Dilone lost the debate and was tossed out. That was followed by a shot by Eldridge down third, but third base umpire Steve Rackley ruled it foul to the dismay of Colborn and the capacity crowd. During the resulting disarray, first base umpire Cory Erickson warned Whitecaps' mascot Crash to stop "inciting" the crowd by using an eye chart to mock the call. Forced to leave his perch on the Whitecaps' dugout roof, Crash stormed off on a wave of boos.

"These are young umpires, and they're developing also," Colborn said. "If Cory feels that's the way he should handle things by going after the mascot, then so be it. That's his choice."

Rockford manager John Mizerock, who was swept in the divisional playoffs last year by South Bend, had some encouraging words for the Whitecaps. "They're a good team, and there's no doubt about that," Mizcrock said. "They have a bunch of guys who can hit and a bunch of guys who can run. Their pitching has been good all year."

Farewell

The season was officially over, and the confetti was being swept away.

There was a sense of urgency among the Whitecaps after that final loss. Activity around the clubhouse resembled factory workers anticipating the five o'clock whistle. Everyone had plans for the offseason.

Several players, including Mat Reese, were heading back to finish college. "I'm going back to Indiana State to earn the last fourteen credits toward my degree in education," Reese said. "I'm going to work out and stay in shape and get ready for next season."

Pitcher Scott Baldwin anticipated reuniting with his wife and going elk hunting, in that order. George Williams, who was in West Michigan basically to rehab his shoulder, was having a home built in Lacrosse, Wisconsin, and he was ready to watch that take shape.

A few players, like Brian Eldridge, expected to get jobs during the offseason. "I'll still have to pay the bills," Eldridge said. "When I'm not working, I'll find time to relax and continue to stay in shape for spring training."

Wedding bells rang for Ryan Whitaker in September. Bill King got married in December.

Vinny Francisco, who had a son during the season, would be moving to Iowa with his wife and Vinny Jr. Juan Dilone and Fred Soriano planned to play winter ball in the Dominican Republic. So did Jason McDonald and Steve Cox.

Catcher Mark Moore wanted to keep his offseason simple. "I'm going to reflect and just hang out," Moore said.

Jim Colborn was already reflective, assessing his first season as a manager: "It was pretty successful. I learned which concepts of the game will work and which ones won't to a certain degree. I'm still in kindergarten, but I at least saw the curriculum for elementary school."

Wait Till Next Year

Jim Colborn was so happy with the news that his smile could be felt right through the telephone.

"Your job and the pay is what people believe is important, but what's really important is the kind of people you work with," said Colborn from his home in Ventura, Cal-

Jason McDonald prepares to head home after the Whitecaps' inaugural season. Courtesy the *Grand Rapids Press*.

ifornia. "The Whitecaps staff and the fans of West Michigan are the kind of great people I love to be around."

Colborn would be around a little longer. In October the Oakland Athletics and the West Michigan Whitecaps announced the field staff for 1995. Colborn would be back after managing the Whitecaps to the first round of the 1994 Midwest League playoffs.

West Michigan general manager Scott Lane was ecstatic about the return of Colborn. "He makes things so easy for us on the staff," Lane said. "He's easy to work with, he's good with the media, and I like his aggressive baseball style."

The Whitecaps also brought back Midwest League trainer of the year Brian Thorson. But pitching coach Gil Patterson, whose pitching staff finished second in the league, wouldn't be back. Patterson was replaced by Bert Bradley, who was pitching coach at Class AAA Tacoma last season.

Keith Lieppman, director of player development for the Oakland club, was the main catalyst in deciding the movement throughout the A's minor league system. "The organization was really pleased with the work done by Colborn and Patterson," Lieppman said. "We moved Gil because he requested to move to Arizona (to Scottsdale, Oakland's Rookie level) for personal reasons. He was in line to get moved up, but he felt at this point it was more important to go to Scottsdale."

Lieppman was also pleased with Bradley. Bradley first joined Oakland in 1979, when the A's drafted him in the twenty-seventh round. In his final year as a pitcher in the Pacific Coast League (Class AAA) he led the league with sixty-five appearances and a 2.76 ERA. He played only one year on the major league level. In 1983, the right-handed relief pitcher earned no decisions in six games pitched.

Bradley was known as part of the 1984 blockbuster trade sending him along with Rickey Henderson to the New York Yankees for Jay Howell, Jose Rijo, Stan Javier, and Eric Plunk.

After his playing career ended, Bradley rejoined the A's as a pitching coach at Madison from 1987-90. He spent 1991-92 in Huntsville and the past two years in Tacoma. "He was sent to West Michigan because of personal reasons. He wanted to be closer to home," Lieppman said. Born in Athens, Georgia, Bradley resides in Toledo, Illinois.

"He's been a really good organizational coach," Lieppman said. "He's been traveling with us so much over the past few years. For the past two years he's worked for us in the Dominican. He's there again right now"

Jim Colborn looked forward to working with the new pitching coach. "I'll miss Gil," Colborn said. "But I know Bert fairly well from working with him in spring training. (When it comes to preparing pitchers) Bert's a little meaner. He's a tough guy."

◆ ◆ ◆

In November Whitecaps general manager Scott Lane was named *The Sporting News* executive of the year. Awarded by the magazine since 1936 in each minor league classification, the honor was combined in 1991 to cover all minor league levels. Lane was the first Class A executive to win.

"A more accurate name for it would be staff of the year," Lane said. "Obviously, it takes more than one person to accomplish what we did. If I take credit for one thing, it would be putting together a staff who shared my dream of becoming the finest organization in minor league baseball. They took that dream and ran with it."

Lane had just finished his seventh season in minor league baseball. He spent the previous three years as assistant general manager of the Kane County Cougars. From 1988-90, he held the same title with the Rockford franchise.

"The West Michigan Whitecaps wouldn't have existed if

In West Michigan the Whitecaps were Number One from start to finish. Courtesy the *Grand Rapids Press*.

not for Lou (Chamberlin) and Denny (Baxter) having the dream," Lane said. "Most of all, I'd like to share the award with the fans of West Michigan who came out in record numbers."

Sporting News senior editor Mark Newman noted that the success in Grand Rapids symbolized the success of the minors in 1994. Whitecaps manager Jim Colborn agreed. "The fans of West Michigan truly deserve the award. Of course, Scott Lane and the staff attracted them, but the people that showed up is what did it."

Colborn considered the honor an obvious choice. "This is the first of many awards that organization should get. They put on the best show in minor league baseball." And who could argue with that?

Player Profiles

Vinny Francisco and Jason McDonald exchange high fives.
Courtesy the *Grand Rapids Press*.

30   SCOTT BALDWIN   Pitcher

Obtained: Selected in the 13th round of the June 1993 free agent draft — graduated from Lewiston HS in 1988 — graduated from Lewis-Clark State College in 1993.

1994 TOTALS

W	L	S	ERA	GP	IP	H	AB	AVG	TBF	R	ER	HR	BB	SO	WP	BK
7	8	1	3.45	25	112.1	90	414	.217	491	55	43	3	62	112	13	6

15   JASON BEVERLIN   Pitcher

Obtained: Selected in the fourth round of the June 1994 free agent draft — graduated from Royal Oak Dondero HS in 1991 — attended Western Carolina University.

1994 TOTALS

W	L	S	ERA	GP	IP	H	AB	AVG	TBF	R	ER	HR	BB	SO	WP	BK
3	2	1	1.76	17	41.0	32	151	.212	168	12	8	0	14	48	3	4

21   TIM BOJAN   Pitcher

Obtained: Selected in the 36th round of the June 1992 free agent draft — graduated from Lincoln Way HS in 1988 — attended the College of St. Francis.

1994 TOTALS

W	L	S	ERA	GP	IP	H	AB	AVG	TBF	R	ER	HR	BB	SO	WP	BK
7	3	3	3.28	38	82.1	56	289	.194	361	44	30	4	60	80	2	2

36   GUSTAVO GIL   Pitcher

Obtained: Signed as a free agent, November 18, 1992. Originally signed by the Montreal Expos on July 16, 1990 — was released during the 1991 season and signed with Oakland following the 1992 season.

1994 TOTALS

W	L	S	ERA	GP	IP	H	AB	AVG	TBF	R	ER	HR	BB	SO	WP	BK
2	8	0	5.02	23	80.2	97	321	.302	361	50	45	11	28	50	6	1

32   AL GOGOLIN   Pitcher

Obtained: Selected in the 13th round of the June 1994 free agent draft — graduated from Marist HS — attended Georgia Tech.

1994 TOTALS

W	L	S	ERA	GP	IP	H	AB	AVG	TBF	R	ER	HR	BB	SO	WP	BK
0	0	1	1.47	11	18.1	13	67	.194	83	6	3	0	14	23	0	2

16   BRENDAN HAUSE   Pitcher

Obtained: Selected in the 37th round of the June 1992 free agent draft — graduated from Mira Mesa HS in 1992.

1994 TOTALS

W	L	S	ERA	GP	IP	H	AB	AVG	TBF	R	ER	HR	BB	SO	WP	BK
0	1	0	5.40	4	13.1	16	49	.327	59	9	8	1	6	5	0	0

35 BILL KING   Pitcher

Obtained: Selected in the third round of the June 1994 free agent draft — graduated from Carroll HS — attended Birmingham-Southern University.

1994 TOTALS

W	L	S	ERA	GP	IP	H	AB	AVG	TBF	R	ER	HR	BB	SO	WP	BK
2	1	4	1.81	17	44.2	35	160	.219	183	11	9	2	19	25	0	1

34 TIM KUBINSKI   Pitcher

Obtained: Selected in the seventh round of the June 1993 free agent draft — graduated from San Luis Obispo HS in 1990 — attended UCLA.

1994 TOTALS

W	L	S	ERA	GP	IP	H	AB	AVG	TBF	R	ER	HR	BB	SO	WP	BK
14	6	0	3.63	30	158.2	168	617	.272	677	82	64	8	36	126	8	10

33 DEREK MANNING Pitcher

Obtained: Selected in the 26th round of the June 1993 free agent draft — graduated from New Hanover HS in 1988 — graduated from the University of North Carolina in 1993.

1994 TOTALS

W	L	S	ERA	GP	IP	H	AB	AVG	TBF	R	ER	HR	BB	SO	WP	BK
11	7	2	2.28	29	154.0	120	564	.213	617	52	39	4	42	118	3	3

20 JASON RAJOTTE Pitcher

Obtained: Selected in the 11th round of the June 1993 free agent draft — graduated from West Warwick HS in 1990 — attended the University of Maine.

1994 TOTALS

W	L	S	ERA	GP	IP	H	AB	AVG	TBF	R	ER	HR	BB	SO	WP	BK
0	4	7	4.15	36	47.2	47	184	.255	208	28	22	0	20	31	2	1

37 ZACK SAWYER Pitcher

Obtained: Selected in the 10th round of the June 1991 free agent draft — graduated from Clinton HS in 1991.

1994 TOTALS

W	L	S	ERA	GP	IP	H	AB	AVG	TBF	R	ER	HR	BB	SO	WP	BK
4	5	3	3.44	40	86.1	66	318	.208	377	41	33	6	49	79	8	3

19 MATT WALSH Pitcher

Obtained: Selected in the 41st round of the June 1993 free agent draft — graduated from Boston College HS in 1990 — attended the University of Rochester before transferring to Boston College.

1994 TOTALS

W	L	S	ERA	GP	IP	H	AB	AVG	TBF	R	ER	HR	BB	SO	WP	BK
10	5	1	3.43	30	133.2	118	499	.236	547	62	51	9	38	98	4	5

12 RYAN WHITAKER Pitcher

Obtained: Selected in the 27th round of the June 1993 free agent draft — graduated from Union HS in 1990 — attended the University of Arkansas.

1994 TOTALS

W	L	S	ERA	GP	IP	H	AB	AVG	TBF	R	ER	HR	BB	SO	WP	BK
3	4	2	4.10	37	79.0	83	312	.266	345	41	36	7	25	56	5	1

10 TONY BANKS Outfielder

Obtained: Selected in the 21st round of the June 1993 free agent draft — graduated from Skyline HS in 1989 — attended Cal State Fullerton.

1994 TOTALS

AVG	AB	R	H	2B	3B	HR	RBI	BB	SO	SB	CS	GDP
.212	245	31	52	15	1	6	27	30	52	8	4	2

27 STEVEN COX   First Base

Obtained: Selected in the fifth round of the June 1992 free agent draft — graduated from Monache HS in 1992.

1994 TOTALS

AVG	AB	R	H	2B	3B	HR	RBI	BB	SO	SB	CS	GDP
.241	311	37	75	19	2	6	32	41	95	2	6	5

31 D. T. CROMER   First Base/Outfielder

Obtained: Selected in the 11th round of the June 1992 free agent draft — graduated from Lexington HS in 1989 — attended the University of South Carolina.

1994 TOTALS

AVG	AB	R	H	2B	3B	HR	RBI	BB	SO	SB	CS	GDP
.255	349	50	89	20	5	10	58	33	76	11	10	5

11   JUAN DILONE   Infielder

Obtained: Signed as a free agent, June 5, 1990.

1994 TOTALS

AVG	AB	R	H	2B	3B	HR	RBI	BB	SO	SB	CS	GDP
.230	352	66	81	15	5	12	48	46	110	29	12	3

14   BRIAN ELDRIDGE   Infielder

Obtained: Selected in the 13th round of the June 1992 free agent draft — graduated from James Monroe HS in 1988 — attended the University of Oklahoma.

1994 TOTALS

AVG	AB	R	H	2B	3B	HR	RBI	BB	SO	SB	CS	GDP
.261	184	28	48	11	1	1	15	17	29	3	0	3

13   VICENTE FRANCISCO   Infielder

Obtained: Signed as a free agent, January 15, 1990.

1994 TOTALS

AVG	AB	R	H	2B	3B	HR	RBI	BB	SO	SB	CS	GDP
.248	452	43	112	19	0	0	41	40	69	16	16	4

25   DAVID KEEL   Outfielder

Obtained: Selected in the 23rd round of the June 1992 free agent draft — graduated from Lee HS in 1990 — attended Motlow State Community College.

1994 TOTALS

AVG	AB	R	H	2B	3B	HR	RBI	BB	SO	SB	CS	GDP
.214	224	32	48	12	4	3	30	50	46	11	7	9

4 ERIC MARTINS Infielder

Obtained: Selected in the 17th round of the 1994 free agent draft — attended Long Beach State University.

1994 TOTALS

AVG	AB	R	H	2B	3B	HR	RBI	BB	SO	SB	CS	GDP
.310	71	11	22	4	1	0	7	5	12	1	2	2

23 JASON McDONALD Outfielder

Obtained: Selected in the fourth round of the June 1993 free agent draft — graduated from Elk Grove HS in 1990 — attended the University of Houston.

1994 TOTALS

AVG	AB	R	H	2B	3B	HR	RBI	BB	SO	SB	CS	GDP
.238	404	67	96	11	9	2	31	81	87	52	23	5

25   MARK MOORE   Catcher

Obtained: Selected in the 50th round of the June 1992 free agent draft — graduated from Shawnee Mission HS East in 1988 — attended Oral Roberts University.

1994 TOTALS

AVG	AB	R	H	2B	3B	HR	RBI	BB	SO	SB	CS	GDP
.274	340	49	93	27	2	9	53	42	79	2	3	10

3   WILLIE MORALES   Catcher

Obtained: Selected in the 14th round of the June 1993 free agent draft — graduated from Tucson HS in 1990 — attended the University of Arizona.

1994 TOTALS

AVG	AB	R	H	2B	3B	HR	RBI	BB	SO	SB	CS	GDP
.266	380	47	101	26	0	13	51	36	64	3	5	12

18   RANDY ORTEGA   Catcher

Obtained: Selected in the 33rd round of the June 1993 free agent draft — graduated from Lincoln HS in 1990 — attended the University of Santa Clara.

1994 TOTALS

AVG	AB	R	H	2B	3B	HR	RBI	BB	SO	SB	CS	GDP
.239	222	26	53	11	0	2	30	29	42	3	0	3

17   MAT REESE   Outfielder

Obtained: Selected in the 16th round of the June 1993 free agent draft — graduated from Maricopa HS in 1989 — attended Indiana State University.

1994 TOTALS

AVG	AB	R	H	2B	3B	HR	RBI	BB	SO	SB	CS	GDP
.258	298	45	77	21	2	2	43	42	70	7	5	6

6   FRED SORIANO   Infielder

Obtained: Signed as an undrafted free agent, February 13, 1992.

1994 TOTALS

AVG	AB	R	H	2B	3B	HR	RBI	BB	SO	SB	CS	GDP
.224	201	30	45	2	1	1	16	21	70	23	7	3

9   GEORGE WILLIAMS   Catcher/Designated Hitter

Obtained: Selected in the 24th round of the June 1991 free agent draft — graduated from Central HS in 1937 — graduated from the University of Texas-Pan American in 1991 — member of the A's 40-man roster.

1994 TOTALS

AVG	AB	R	H	2B	3B	HR	RBI	BB	SO	SB	CS	GDP
.303	221	40	67	20	1	8	48	44	47	6	3	3

BOB BENNETT   Pitcher

Promoted to Modesto on May 5.

1994 TOTALS

W	L	S	ERA	GP	IP	H	AB	AVG	TBF	R	ER	HR	BB	SO	WP	BK
0	2	1	2.19	6	24.2	23	93	.247	103	8	6	1	6	23	0	0

STEVE LEMKE   Pitcher

Promoted to Modesto on May 24. Midwest League Pitcher of the Week, May 8-May 14.

1994 TOTALS

W	L	S	ERA	GP	IP	H	AB	AVG	TBF	R	ER	HR	BB	SO	WP	BK
4	2	1	2.27	10	43.2	38	168	.226	180	13	11	1	6	29	2	0

CHRIS MICHALAK   Pitcher

Promoted to Modesto on June 21.

1994 TOTALS

W	L	S	ERA	GP	IP	H	AB	AVG	TBF	R	ER	HR	BB	SO	WP	BK
5	3	0	3.90	15	67.0	66	249	.265	291	32	29	3	28	38	2	3

WILLIAM URBINA   Pitcher

Sent to Arizona for rehab (torn anterior cruciate ligament) on May 21. Had surgery in August.

1994 TOTALS

W	L	S	ERA	GP	IP	H	AB	AVG	TBF	R	ER	HR	BB	SO	WP	BK
0	2	0	13.90	6	6.2	18	35	.514	46	16	14	1	9	3	0	0

STEVE ZONGOR Pitcher

Promoted to Modesto on June 18.

1994 TOTALS

W	L	S	ERA	GP	IP	H	AB	AVG	TBF	R	ER	HR	BB	SO	WP	BK
2	1	9	2.38	22	22.2	11	76	.145	93	6	6	0	13	26	3	0

JEFF D'AMICO Shortstop

Placed on DL with torn anterior cruciate ligament on April 24. Had surgery on June 27.

1994 TOTALS

AVG	AB	R	H	2B	3B	HR	RBI	BB	SO	SB	CS	GDP
.278	36	5	10	3	0	0	3	4	7	2	2	0

MARCEL GALLIGANI   Outfielder

Released on June 25.

1994 TOTALS

AVG	AB	R	H	2B	3B	HR	RBI	BB	SO	SB	CS	GDP
.207	116	12	24	5	0	3	15	15	44	3	3	1

JOSE GUILLEN   Infielder

Promoted to Modesto on May 15.

1994 TOTALS

AVG	AB	R	H	2B	3B	HR	RBI	BB	SO	SB	CS	GDP
.225	102	18	23	4	1	0	10	20	24	9	4	1

ALL PITCHERS

1994 TOTALS

W	L	S	ERA	GP	IP	H	AVG	R	ER	HR	BB	SO	WP
74	65	36	3.42	139	1220.0	1103	.241	577	464	61	483	971	61

ALL BATTERS

1994 TOTALS

AVG	AB	R	H	2B	3B	HR	RBI	BB	SO	SB	CS	E
.248	4508	637	1116	245	35	78	558	596	1023	191	112	221

Team Statistics

West Michigan Whitecaps
Day-By-Day Attendance, April 12–September 2, 1994

Bold indicates sold out game. Figures include lawn seating tickets sold.

Date	Attendance	Date	Attendance
April 12	**6,210**	May 21	**6,883**
April 13	3,639	May 26	6,062
April 14	4,427	May 27	6,711
April 15	4,708	May 28	**7,154**
April 16	**5,938**	May 29	**7,140**
April 17	**5,960**	June 7	6,211
April 27	4,874	June 8	6,710
April 28	RAINED OUT	June 11	**7,513**
April 29	5,900	June 12	**7,491**
April 30	5,797	June 13	6,730
May 1	5,776	June 14	6,765
May 2	4,671	June 15	6,694
May 11	5,926	June 16	6,864
May 12	6,240	June 17	7,301
May 13	6,515	June 18	**7,791**
May 14	**6,704**	June 30	**7,825**
May 15	6,198	July 1	7,113
May 16	6,027	July 2	**8,022**
May 17	6,099	July 3	7,250
May 18	6,164	July 4	6,771
May 20	**6,871**	July 5	6,513

July 6	6,961	August 13	**8,136**
July 7	7,805	August 14	**8,135**
July 13	7,308	August 15	**8,134**
July 14	6,697	August 16	**8,156**
July 15	7,948	August 24	**8,170**
July 16	**8,114**	August 25	**8,156**
July 17	**8,145**	August 26	**8,154**
July 18	7,219	August 27	**8,200**
July 19	7,547	August 28	**8,145**
July 20	7,413	August 29	7,906
August 1	**8,118**	August 30	RAINED OUT
August 2	**8,140**	August 31	**8,183**
August 9	**8,149**	Sept. 1	**8,168**
August 10	7,652	Sept. 2	**8,195**

Total: 475,212

Top 20 Season-Long Attendance Totals
Class A Professional Baseball, 1901-1994

1.	1994	**West Michigan Whitecaps**	**Midwest League**	**475,212**
2.	1949	Denver Bears	Western League	463,039
3.	1952	Denver Bears	Western League	461,419
4.	1951	Denver Bears	Western League	424,065
5.	1994	Kane County Cougars	Midwest League	417,744
6.	1994	Rancho Cucamonga Quakes	California League	386,633
7.	1950	Denver Bears	Western League	379,180
8.	1994	Lake Elsinore Storm	California League	357,123
9.	1993	Kane County Cougars	Midwest League	354,327
10.	1993	Frederick Keys	Carolina League	351,146
11.	1994	Frederick Keys	Carolina League	344,563
12.	1994	Wilmington Blue Rocks	Carolina League	335,024
13.	1993	Wilmington Blue Rocks	Carolina League	332,132
14.	1993	Rancho Cucamonga Quakes	California League	331,005
15.	1992	Frederick Keys	Carolina League	329,592
16.	1992	Kane County Cougars	Midwest League	323,769
17.	1953	Denver Bears	Western League	322,128
18.	1993	Fort Wayne Wizards	Midwest League	318,506
19.	1991	Frederick Keys	Carolina League	318,354
20.	1993	Durham Bulls	Carolina League	305,692

Compiled from *The Encyclopedia of Minor League Baseball,*
Baseball America Inc.

1994 National Association of Professional Baseball Leagues
Top 20 Official Regular Season Attendance

(compiled from Howe Sportsdata International reports)

Team	League	Attendance	Dates	Avg.
1. Buffalo Bisons	AAA — American Association	982,493	70	14,036
2. Salt Lake Buzz	AAA — Pacific Coast League	713,224	70	10,189
3. Ottawa Lynx	AAA — International League	596,858	67	8,901
4. Louisville Redbirds	AAA — American Association	573,174	70	8,188
5. Norfolk Tides	AAA — International League	546,826	67	8,162
6. Columbus Clippers	AAA — International League	535,145	69	7,756
7. Richmond Braves	AAA — International League	507,322	68	7,461
8. Scranton-WB Red Barons	AAA — International League	476,042	66	7,213
9. Iowa Cubs	AAA — American Association	485,734	68	7,143
10. West Michigan Whitecaps	**A — Midwest League**	**475,212**	**68**	**6,988**
11. Birmingham Barons	AA — Southern League	467,868	67	6,983
12. Pawtucket Red Sox	AAA — International League	469,029	70	6,700
13. Omaha Royals	AAA — American Association	439,277	68	6,460
14. Kane County Cougars	A — Midwest League	417,744	67	6,235

1994 National Association of Professional Baseball Leagues
Top 20 Official Regular Season Attendance (continued)

15.	San Antonio Missions	AA — Texas League	411,959	67	6,149
16.	Charlotte Knights	AAA — International League	391,730	67	5,847
17.	Rancho Cucamonga Quakes	A — California League	386,633	67	5,771
18.	Trenton Thunder	AA — Eastern League	318,252	57	5,583
19.	Rochester Red Wings	AAA — International League	363,717	66	5,511
20.	Tulsa Drillers	AA — Texas League	344,764	63	5,472

West Michigan Whitecaps
1994 Day-By-Day Results

Date	Opp.	W-L	Score	Record	Place	GB	Winner	Loser	Save
FIRST HALF									
4/8	@SB	L	2-1	0-1	2	1	Proctor	**Kubinski,0-1**	
4/9	@SB	W	10-9	1-1	2	1	**Zongor,1-0**	Bailey	
4/10	@SB	L	8-7	1-2	5	2	Fitzpatrick	**Whitaker,0-1**	
4/11	@SB	Rained Out							
4/12	Bur	W	5-2	2-2	4	1.5	**Michalak,1-0**	Pacheo	
4/13	Bur	W	3-1	3-2	3	1.5	**Kubinski,1-1**	DaSilva	**Bennett,1**
4/14	Bur	L	2-1 (10)	3-3	4	2.5	Bullock	**Lemke,0-1**	Kermode
4/15	Bur	W	5-3	4-3	3	1.5	**Whitaker,1-1**	Schneider	**Zongor,1**
4/16	Roc	W	6-2	5-3	3	1.5	**Michalak,2-0**	Grundy	**Sawyer,1**
4/17	Roc	L	7-4	5-4	3	1.5	Rusch	**Bennett,0-1**	Brewer
4/18	off								
4/19	@Spr	W	3-1	6-4	3	1.5	**Manning,1-0**	Lachappa	
4/20	@Spr	W	7-4	7-4	3	1.5	**Walsh,1-0**	K. White	

198

Date	Opp.	W-L	Score	Record	Place	GB	Winner	Loser	Save
4/21	@Spr	L	5-1	7-5	4	1.5	Baron	**Sawyer,0-1**	Schlutt
4/22	@Spr	L	6-5	7-6	5	2	White	**Zongor,1-1**	
4/23	@CR	L	6-5	7-7	7	3	Slade	**Lemke,0-2**	Drysdale
4/24	@CR	L	15-3	7-8	6	4	Perisho	**Bojan,0-1**	
4/25	@CR	W	3-2	8-8	5	4	**Sawyer,1-1**	Edsell	**Walsh,1**
4/26	@CR	L	13-2	8-9	6	4	Lloyd	**Bennett,0-2**	
4/27	Peo	W	3-2	9-9	6	3	**Lemke,1-2**	Hillman	**Manning,1**
4/28	Peo			Rained Out					
4/29	Mad	W	4-0	10-9	5	2.5	**Bojan,1-1**	Ottmers	**Baldwin,1**
4/30	Mad	W	8-6	11-9	5	2.5	**Kubinski,2-1**	Sailors	**Zongor,2**
5/1	Mad	W	1-0	12-9	5	2	**Walsh,2-0**	Davis	
5/2	Mad	L	7-6	12-10	5	3	Windham	**Urbina,0-1**	
5/3	@Bel	L	4-3	12-11	5	4	Salmon	**Bojan,1-2**	Salmon
5/4	@Bel	W	7-5	13-11	5	3	**Sawyer,2-1**	Schmitt	
5/5	@Peo	W	5-4	14-11	5	3	**Lemke,2-2**	Lopez	
5/6	@Pec	L	1-0	14-12	5	3	Bobbitt	**Rajotte,0-1**	
5/7	@Cli	L	11-10(10)	14-13	5	4	Martin	**Whitaker,1-2**	
5/8	@Cli	L	17-3	14-14	6	4	Altman	**Sawyer,2-2**	

199

Date	Opp.	W-L	Score	Record	Place	GB	Winner	Loser	Save
5/9	@Cli	L	5-2	14-15	6	4	Altman	**Kubinski,2-2**	
5/10	@Cli	W	8-2	15-15	6	3	**Lemke,3-2**	Brewington	
5/11	QC	L	6-2	15-16	7	4	Walker	**Baldwin,0-1**	Barrios
5/12	QC	L	5-1	15-17	7	5	Wagner	**Michalak,2-1**	Westbrook
5/13	QC	W	3-1	16-17	7	5	**Kubinski,3-2**	Czanstkowski	
5/14	QC	W	4-2	17-17	6	4.5	**Lemke,4-2**	Blanco	**Manning,2**
5/15	KC	L	4-2(11)	17-18	6	6	Walania	**Baldwin,0-2**	
5/16	KC	L	8-5(14)	17-19	6	6	Filbeck	**Urbina,0-2**	
5/17	KC	L	8-3	17-20	7	6.5	Alfonseca	**Walsh,2-1**	
5/18	KC	W	6-5	18-20	7	5.5	**Manning,2-0**	Walania	**Lemke,1**
5/19	off								
5/20	FtW	W	9-0	19-20	6	6	**Baldwin,1-2**	Perkins	**Bojan,1**
5/21	FtW	L	5-2	19-21	7	7	Linebarger	**Michalak,2-2**	Boewers
5/22	@Roc	W	3-2	20-21	7	5.5	**Kubinski,4-2**	Burley	**Zongor,3**
5/24	@Roc	L	4-1	20-22	7	6.5	Rowitzer	**Manning,2-1**	Atkinson
5/24	@Roc	W	9-4	21-22	7	6	**Baldwin,2-2**	Rusch	
5/25	@Roc	W	5-1	22-22	7	6	**Michalak,3-2**	Grundy	
5/26	SB	W	4-1	23-22	5	4	**Kubinski,5-2**	Eyre	**Whitaker,1**

Date	Opp.	W-L	Score	Record	Place	GB	Winner	Loser	Save
5/26	SB	W	2-0	24-22	5	4	**Bojan,2-2**	Fitzpatrick	**Zongor,4**
5/27	SB	L	3-0	24-23	t6	4.5	Sirotka	**Walsh,2-2**	
5/28	SB	L	9-3	24-24	7	5.5	Lindemann	**Baldwin,2-3**	
5/29	SB	W	11-4	25-24	t6	5.5	Woods	**Manning,2-2**	
5/30	@App	W	4-3	26-24	t6	4.5	**Michalak,4-2**	Hinchliffe	**Zongor,5**
5/31	@App	L	3-2(10)	26-25	7	5.5	Krueger	**Whitaker,1-3**	
6/1	@App	L	4-3	26-26	7	6.5	Franklin	**Rajotte,0-1**	
6/2	@App	L	5-1	26-27	7	7.5	Smith	**Baldwin,2-4**	
6/3	@KC	L	2-1	26-28	7	8.5	Valdes	**Manning,2-3**	
6/4	@KC	L	3-1	26-29	7	9.5	Ehler	**Michalak,4-3**	Rich
6/5	@KC	W	16-2	27-29	7	9.5	**Kubinski,6-2**	Mays	
6/6	@KC	L	8-3	27-30	7	10.5	Larkin	**Walsh,2-3**	
6/7	FtW	W	2-1	28-30	7	9.5	**Gil,1-0**	Tatar	**Zongor,6**
6/8	FtW	L	5-2(13)	28-31	7	9.5	O'Brien	**Sawyer,2-3**	Linebarger
6/9	@FtW	W	10-3	29-31	7	9.5	**Michalak,5-3**	Perkins	
6/10	@FtW	L	2-0	29-32	7	10.5	DeJesus	**Kubinski,6-3**	
6/11	App	W	7-6	30-32	7	9.5	**Walsh,3-3**	Franklin	**Zongor,7**
6/12	App	W	3-2	31-32	7	9.5	**Baldwin,3-4**	Smith	**Zongor,8**

Date	Opp.	W-L	Score	Record	Place	GB	Winner	Loser	Save
6/13	App	L	6-3	31-33	7	10	Monane	**Manning,2-4**	Mantei
6/14	App	W	4-3	32-33	7	9.5	**Bojan,3-2**	Cope	**Zongor,9**
6/15	Bel	W	7-6(11)	33-33	7	10	**Zongor,2-1**	Wilstead	
6/16	Bel	L	6-1	33-34	t7	11	Kopitzke	**Walsh,3-4**	
6/17	Bel	W	3-2	34-34	6	10	**Baldwin,4-4**	Wunsch	**Bojan, 2**
6/18	Bel	L	4-2	34-35	6	11	Wilstead	**Bojan,3-3**	Maloney
6/19-21	All-Star Break								

SECOND HALF

Date	Opp.	W-L	Score	Record	Place	GB	Winner	Loser	Save
6/22	@Burl	W	9-3	1-0	t1	-	**Kubinski,7-3**	Markham	
6/23	@Burl	Rained Out							
6/24G1	@Burl	L	3-1	1-1	t2	1	DaSilva	**Manning,3-4**	
6/24G2	@Burl	W	8-4	2-1	t2	1	**Baldwin,5-4**	Phelps	
6/25	@Burl	L	7-5 (10)	2-2	2	1	Pacheco	**Sawyer,2-4**	
6/26	@QC	W	8-6	3-2	4	1	**Beverlin,1-0**	Walter	**Rajotte,1**
6/27	@QC	W	11-1	4-2	t2	1	**Kubinski,8-3**	Grzanich	**Gogolin,1**
6/28	@QC	W	5-2	5-2	t1	-	**Baldwin,6-4**	Walker	**Rajotte,2**
6/29	@QC	W	7-5	6-2	1	+1	**Manning,4-4**	Lewis	

Date	Opp.	W-L	Score	Record	Place	GB	Winner	Loser	Save
6/30	Spr	W	4-2	7-2	1	+1	**Walsh,4-4**	Arroyo	**Bojan,3**
7/1	Spr	L	2-1	7-3	t1	-	Kaufman	**Gil,1-1**	Wolf
7/2	Spr	W	8-4	8-3	1	-	**Kubinski,9-3**	Duran	
7/3	Spr	L	6-2	8-4	1	+1	Kindler	**Baldwin,6-5**	Wolf
7/4	CR	W	3-2 (11)	9-4	1	+1	**Bojan,4-3**	DeClue	
7/5	CR	W	8-4	10-4	1	+1	**Walsh,5-4**	Lloyd	**Whitaker,2**
7/6	CR	L	5-4	10-5	t1	-	Edsell	**Gil,1-2**	
7/7	CR	W	14-5	11-5	1	+.5	**King,1-0**	Fontano	
7/8	@Blt	W	3-2	12-5	1	+1.5	**Baldwin,7-5**	Wagner	**Sawyer, 2**
7/9	@Blt	W	12-4	13-5	1	+2	**Manning,5-4**	Wunsch	
7/10	@Blt	L	3-2	13-6	1	+1	Sadler	**Beverlin,1-1**	
7/11	@Blt	L	10-7	13-7	t1	-	Cole	**Gil,1-3**	
7/12	off								
7/13	Roc	L	9-4(11)	13-8	2	-1	Brewer	**Sawyer,2-5**	
7/14	Roc	L	5-0	13-9	4	-2	Smith	**Baldwin,7-6**	
7/15	Roc	W	2-0	14-9	t4	-1	**Manning,6-4**	Ray	**King,1**
7/16	Roc	W	6-2	15-9	2	-1	**Walsh,6-4**	Grundy	**Rajotte,3**
7/17	Cli	W	12-4	16-9	2	-1	**Gil,2-3**	Charlton	

203

Date	Opp.	W-L	Score	Record	Place	GB	Winner	Loser	Save
7/18	Cli	W	8-2	17-9	2	-1	**Kubinski,10-3**	Bourgeois	
7/19	Cli	L	3-2	17-10	2	-2	Myers	**Baldwin,7-7**	
7/20	Cli	W	4-0 (5)	18-10	2	-1.5	**Manning,7-4**	Hicks	
7/21	@App	W	14-4	19-10	2	-1.5	**Walsh,7-4**	Estes	
7/22	@App	L	7-2	19-11	2	-2.5	Smith	**Gil,2-4**	
7/23	@App	L	4-1	19-12	2	-2.5	Sanchez	**Kubinski,10-4**	Mantei
7/24	@App	L	14-2	19-13	2	-3.5	Montane	**Baldwin,7-8**	
7/25	@KC	L	2-0	19-14	t2	-3.5	Cunnane	**Manning,7-5**	
7/26	@KC	L	7-4	19-15	3	-3.5	Rich	**Beverlin,1-2**	
7/27	@Roc	L	8-7 (13)	19-16	4	-4	Atkinson	**McDonald,0-1**	
7/28	@Roc	L	4-3	19-17	t4	-4	Hodges	**Kubinski,10-5**	
7/29	@Roc	L	5-4	19-18	t5	-4	Smith	**Rajotte,0-3**	
7/30	@Roc	L	1-0	19-19	6	-5	Ray	**Manning,7-6**	
8/1	App	W	6-4	20-19	5	-5	**Walsh,8-4**	Cole	Zongor,4
8/2	App	L	1-0	20-20	5	-5.5	Smith	**Gil,2-5**	Mantei
8/3	@Peo	L	8-2	20-21	5	-5.5	Stephenson	**Kubinski,10-6**	
8/4	@Peo	W	7-5	21-21	5	-4.5	**King,2-0**	Culberson	Rajotte,4
8/5	@Mad	W	6-1	22-21	5	-4.5	**Manning,8-6**	Davis	

204

Date	Opp.	W-L	Score	Record	Place	GB	Winner	Loser	Save
8/6	@Mad	W	6-5	23-21	5	-4.5	**Beverlin,2-2**	Matulevich	**Rajotte,5**
8/7	@Mad	L	9-6	23-22	5	-5.5	Windham	**Gil,2-6**	Matulevich
8/8	@Mad	W	4-2	24-22	4	-5.5	**Kubinski,11-6**	Detmers	**King,2**
8/9	KC	W	4-0	25-22	4	-5.0	**Bojan,5-3**	Thornton	
8/10	KC	L	1-0	25-23	4	-5.5	Cunnane	**Manning,8-7**	
8/11	@FtW	W	9-2	26-23	4	-4.0	**Walsh,9-4**	Ruch	
8/12	@FtW	L	6-4	26-24	4	-5.0	Miller	**Gil,2-7**	O'Brien
8/13	SB	W	9-1	27-24	4	-5.0	**Kubinski,12-6**	McCormack	
8/14	SB	W	10-2	28-24	4	-5.0	**Manning,9-7**	Lehman	
8/15	PEO	L	3-0	28-25	4	-5.0	Culberson	**Whitaker,1-4**	
8/16	PEO	L	7-3	28-26	5	-6.0	Hillman	**King,2-1**	
8/17	@FtW	L	8-5	28-27	5	-7.0	Lehoisky	**Rajotte,0-4**	
8/18	@FtW	W	6-3	29-27	5	-7.0	**Kubinski,13-6**	O'Brien	
8/19	@SE	W	8-2 (6 inn)	30-27	t4	-6.0	**Manning,10-7**	Lehman	
8/20	@SB	W	4-1	31-27	4	-6.0	**Whitaker,2-4**	Sirotka	**King,3**
8/21	@SB	L	9-6	31-28	4	-6.0	Fordham	**Walsh,9-5**	Bailey
8/22	@SB	W	7-6	32-28	4	-5.0	**Beverlin,3-2**	Woods	**Rajotte,7**
8/23	off				t3	-5.5			

205

Date	Opp.	W-L	Score	Record	Place	GB	Winner	Loser	Save
8/24	FtW	W	6-4	33-28	3	-5.5	**Kubinski,14-6**	Sampson	**King,4**
8/25	FtW	W	6-3	34-28	3	-5.0	**Bojan,6-3**	Peters	
8/26	KC	W	5-4 (12 inn)	35-28	3	-5.0	**Sawyer,3-5**	Anderson	
8/27	KC	W	3-2 (11 inn)	36-28	3	-5.0	**Sawyer,4-5**	Filbeck	
8/28	Bel	L	3-2	36-29	3	-5.0	Cole	**Hause,0-1**	Maloney
8/29	Bel	W	6-5	37-29	3	-5.0	**Bojan,6-5**	Duda	
8/30	Bel	Rained Out							
8/31G1	Bel	W	6-2	38-29	2	-4.5	**Manning,11-7**	Lidle	
8/31G2	Bel	W	2-0	39-29	2	-4.0	**Whitaker,3-4**	Wagner	**Beverlin,1**
9/1	FtW	W	8-2	40-29	2	-4.0	**Walsh,10-5**	Miller	
9/2	FtW	L	5-3	40-30	2	-5.0	Lehoisky	**Gil,2-8**	DeBrino

END OF REGULAR SEASON